How to Learn
ALMOST
ANYTHING
in 48 H⊙URS

How to Learn
ALMOST
ANYTHING
in 48 HOURS

The Skills You Need to
Work Smarter, Study Faster,
and Remember More!

TANSEL ALI

Adams Media

New York London Toronto Sydney New Delhi

Adams Media
An Imprint of Simon & Schuster, Inc.
100 Technology Center Drive
Stoughton, MA 02072

First published in Australia by Hardie Grant Books
First Adams Media trade paperback edition AUGUST 2016

ADAMS MEDIA and colophon are trademarks of Simon and Schuster.

For information about special discounts for bulk purchases, please contact Simon & Schuster Special Sales at 1-866-506-1949 or business@ simonandschuster.com.

The Simon & Schuster Speakers Bureau can bring authors to your live event. For more information or to book an event contact the Simon & Schuster Speakers Bureau at 1-866-248-3049 or visit our website at www.simonspeakers.com.

Text design by Patrick Cannon
Interior images by Kathy Konkle © Simon & Schuster, Inc.

Manufactured in the United States of America

11 2022

Library of Congress Cataloging-in-Publication Data has been applied for.

ISBN 978-1-4405-9776-3
ISBN 978-1-4405-9777-0 (ebook)

To My Father, Ali

CONTENTS

FOREWORD

Over the next ten years education will be massively disrupted. Everyone will be able to learn anything they want five to ten times faster than they do now. Tansel Ali has already started this disruption, and in *How to Learn Almost Anything in 48 Hours* he introduces us to concepts and techniques that give the reader tools to learn anything in record time. This enjoyable book also provides practical exercises, tools, tips, and tricks to practice these skills not traditionally taught in schools. Congratulations to Tansel for leading the way to faster and better learning, and setting the groundwork for the next decade of education. The future of learning is here.

Nolan Bushnell
Founder of Atari Corporation
March 2015

7-STEP GUIDE TO LEARNING ANYTHING IN 48 HOURS

Following is a seven-step guide to learning almost anything in forty-eight hours. Applied with the techniques and tips from this book, it will create a structured process for you to follow.

1. **Gather materials and resources to learn (up to three hours)**

   You've made the choice to learn something. The first step then is to gather all the resources and materials you need to get started. If you were to learn a language, for example, the list of resources might include books, audio, websites, and apps. It might also be helpful to find a native speaker with whom you can practice speaking the language.

2. **Develop a memorization strategy (up to two hours)**

   Once you have gathered all you need, make a decision on the memory techniques you plan to use from this book. For example, if you want to memorize a lengthy list, such as past presidents of the United States of America, you would look at using the Method of Loci. If you want to acquire knowledge fast, you would look at developing a mind map of the content and using visualization methods such as SMASHIN' SCOPE to create engaging associations in your mind with the knowledge. Reading this book will help with identifying the most relevant strategy. The more practice you get at identifying which memory techniques to use, the better you become at developing a memorization strategy.

3. **Organize/prioritize materials (up to one hour)**

With your strategy developed, the next step is to organize the materials and resources you have to fit inside your strategy. If your strategy was to memorize 1,500 French phrases, then you will need to make sure you have your 1,500 French phrases set out in a way that will make it easy for you to go through them one by one. One method of doing that is to enter or copy and paste each phrase into a spreadsheet so that it becomes easy to access.

4. **Create accountability (up to one hour)**

It is important to share your learning task with a family member, friend, or anyone else who will hold you accountable. Accountability to others creates motivation to get you going so that you don't let others down. We do tend to slack off if we are accountable to only ourselves.

5. **Memorize (up to thirty hours)**

Once you have all of your materials and have developed your process for learning, it is time for action. It is best to start with short periods of memorization rather than long. Why? Because it is less strain on the brain, you will complete a set memorization period quickly, and as you get better you will increase your time. If you start with longer memorization periods it will overwhelm you very quickly. Keep it short and simple.

6. **Review (spaced repetition) (up to one hour)**
    Once you have memorized, go back and review your work. This helps to store your memorization in long-term memory. Depending on what you're learning, of course, the rule for spaced repetition is to review an hour later, then a day later, then a week later, a month later, three months later, six months later, and finally a year later.

7. **Practice and apply (up to ten hours)**
    Once you have memorized and used techniques to achieve what you want, practice giving yourself feedback on your memorization. This is the test of how much you have learned. If you have memorized 1,500 French phrases, go into an environment where French is spoken and have conversations. Are you able to speak it? What works? What doesn't? Learn from your experience and then go back and rememorize. Practicing what you have memorized is crucial to the learning process. Memorization only helps you store the information; learning helps you understand. Practice is the intersection of these two. So try to practice as much as you can and, before you know it, you will learn anything you want to learn in record time.

CHAPTER 1

GETTING STARTED

*"Nothing is impossible—the word itself says
'I'm possible'!"*—Audrey Hepburn

TIME IS PERHAPS the most precious thing we possess. We only have it once, it's not renewable, and we could all use it better. We can be so entrenched in our daily lives that, in spite of our desires, we can't seem to find the time to better ourselves, pursue our hobbies, and participate in activities we love. I frequently hear people say they wish they could learn a language, play a musical instrument, or even hang out with their family more—if only they had the time. But then time passes, and nothing changes. We need to remind ourselves, as many philosophies and religions espouse, that all we have is *now. How to Learn Almost Anything in 48 Hours* gives you new skills to learn things that you never thought possible, and to make sure your time is used effectively.

Today at the touch of a few buttons we have access to far more information than we could ever need. We're not just bombarded with information from online but from schools, universities, workplaces, seminars, workshops, and conferences. Unfortunately, our brains are often unable to cope with the relentless volume of data from multiple sources day after day. Information overload is a real problem and can cause anxiety and stress. Stress may cause increased forgetfulness, and reduced confidence, self-esteem, and productivity. Learning should be exciting and fun and *never* frightening. With that in mind, this book is a deliberate, conscious disruption to traditional learning methods, especially that of rote learning.

Studying memory has made me appreciate that the brain is far more amazing than most of us realize. The idea for *How to Learn Almost Anything in 48 Hours* came about after I memorized two *Yellow Pages* phone books in only twenty-four days. I reasoned that the techniques and strategies that helped me do that could be used by everyone to learn faster and better, and the memory techniques explained here apply to all forms of information-based learning.

No matter what your school grades, class, culture, or environment indicate, I believe you can learn anything you want to. Nothing is too difficult. People who have learned these memory techniques have gone on to learn languages in record time, memorize books, shine as elite athletes, dazzle as public speakers, and become outstanding leaders and people of influence such as inventor and entrepreneur Elon Musk and basketball star LeBron James. You do not require a degree or need to have aced certain exams to have this knowledge. You just need your imagination and the will to try.

KEY POINTS

- Make the most of now. Don't delay starting something. There is only now.
- Think about your personal goals and how you would like to lead your life.
- Your mind is amazing; therefore you have the ability to be amazing.
- Do not be afraid to fail. I'm writing this book *because* I've failed countless times.
- Don't give up. Muhammad Ali was once asked how many sit-ups he could do. He replied that he only started counting once he started to hurt. Pushing through that difficult part will lead to success.

HOW IT WORKS

"The secret of getting ahead is getting started."
—attributed to Mark Twain

DID YOU KNOW?

New brain connections are created
every time you form a memory.

CHAPTER 2

MEMORY PRINCIPLES

IN RECENT YEARS there has been an explosion of interest in all matters to do with the brain, as seen in the popularity of brain apps, books and games, and topics such as plasticity and general brain health gaining greater currency. This book helps you adopt newer, faster, more effective forms of learning, which also means training your brain to think and act in new ways.

Imagination Is the Key

For generations, rote learning has been our principal way of remembering things, with repetition the sole focus of our memorization. A more effective way of remembering, though, is to use your imagination. Rather than repeat information over and over again, create highly imaginative visual stories to connect with what is to be remembered. Aside from being fun, remembering made-up stories engages your brain in many more ways than traditional memorization. Words are processed on one side of the brain, images on the other. Repeating words is ineffective, but creating images from those words is incredibly effective.

Consider how often people go back to reread sentences in books because they felt they missed something or could have understood something better. It happens a lot. Contrast that with people watching a movie and how many would rewind every few minutes to make sure they don't miss anything. I'm guessing there would be none. This is because the movie visually engages us; we see body language, environments, we feel emotion, we experience being in the moment, we are one with the movie. Reading text is different. There needs to be an "encoding" process that transforms the text into images for us to truly understand—we need to create the experience. This doesn't mean that watching something is better than reading. It just means that using visual processes to trigger your imagination helps you remember better. Reading text can also trigger the imagination far beyond what you see on a movie screen. Imagination gives you a better mind and memory to learn faster and better.

Memory Foundation: The Building Blocks to a Better Memory
Before learning memory techniques, it is essential to build a foundation for your memory. Having a foundation gives you the basics to remember and learn anything. Without it you will not learn as effectively and will need to keep going back to review your work. Interestingly, the two major principles discussed in this chapter build both memory foundation skills and creativity; they work hand in hand, complementing each other in the memory process.

SMASHIN' SCOPE

One of the greatest learning methods I've come across in my many years as a memory trainer is called SMASHIN' SCOPE. It was devised by British learning entrepreneur Tony Buzan, who also created mind mapping (more on that later), and his colleague Vanda North. It's an acronym that details how we can use our brain to greatly enhance visual perception. These twelve principles can not only help you remember better; they can help you become a more creative and lateral thinker.

Synesthesia/Senses. This interesting word refers to our senses and sensations. Generally when we picture something it is a static image. If I said "whiteboard," most people will see in their mind's eye a whiteboard—either mounted on a wall or on wheels. Rather than just "seeing" the image, if we use our other senses we can become further engaged and involved with our subject—think of smell, touch, taste, and sound. If you went up to the whiteboard and licked it, what would it taste like? Next time you see static images, use your senses to exercise your mind.

Movement. Movement makes a static image dynamic. Using the whiteboard example, we can now visualize it spinning around, moving from side to side, or even growing legs and walking out of the room. The subject could even be you moving around the object—maybe you're flying around it or vice versa. Movement creates traction in the brain that connects its subject, making it more memorable.

Association. Without association there is no connection. If there is no connection then there is no memory. Visualize a pen next to paper—this is a weak association because there is no physical connection, but if the pen writes on the paper there is a connection. But to make this more exciting and memorable, what if the pen scribbles on the paper, ripping it to shreds? Writing on paper is a very logical and common thing. The shredding story doesn't occur every day so it's more memorable, with the brain saying, "Wow, what just happened?"

Sexuality/Self. Tony Buzan says we all have a good memory around this topic so let's use it. Maybe what you're trying to remember or visualize resembles a certain body part. There are many ways to use this type of imagery for people so inclined. When I'm working with kids, though, I tell them to visualize themselves as the subject: imagine being the actual whiteboard. How does it feel to have people write on your face all day? Do you get a kick out of it or are you stuck and wishing to be free?

Humor. Something funny can be a huge help with your visualizing. This doesn't mean you have to be the funniest person in the room, it means use what's funny to you. When I meet someone called John, for example, I immediately picture him sitting on a toilet. For me that's funny, for others it may not be—but it is memorable. I believe comedians are often super-creative beings because they find ways to communicate a point and to make it entertaining and unique. If you want to exercise your creativity, why not learn more about comedy?

Imagination. When we visualize we usually think of real things in our world. We try to make logical associations with what we are trying to remember: I sat down on the chair; I stopped at the red light; I typed on my laptop. These examples are perfectly normal, but they are not memorable. If we want to have a great memory and become more creative, we need to step outside this logical realm. Instead of just imagining sitting on a chair, how about the chair turning around, jumping, and then sitting on you? Your brain sees this image with stunning clarity precisely because it isn't a normal occurrence, and so a stronger mental image is created. Imagination is your friend that can take you to places and help you see things you have never seen or experienced before. As Victor Hugo so vividly put it: "Imagination is intelligence with an erection."

Numbers. Sometimes we need a bit of order in our visualizations. Numbers create that order and provide some much-needed relief for the logical thinkers among us. Applying numbers that mean something to you to an image can create a much stronger emotional connection to that image. The number 23, for example, reminds me of the great basketball hero Michael Jordan. If I see the number 23 anywhere it reminds me of him and the day my Jordan 5 shoes were stolen while playing football.

Symbolism. As we've heard, a picture is worth a thousand words. Symbols often carry a great deal of information at just a glance. They also help communicate a specific message. What would happen, say, if street signs were written in sentences? You wouldn't have time to read them before another sign appeared, and then another, then *Bang!* you've crashed. Your brain processes images much faster than words, which is exactly how speed-reading works.

Color. Creativity loves color. Used well, colors can help you think and remember very quickly. Instead of visualizing a bright red tomato, perhaps see it as a bright blue tomato. That whiteboard might actually be black and blue, not white and silver. All you need to do is visualize the difference, and that will be enough to make it memorable. But you don't always have to choose a different color to visualize the item. If you use the same color as the thing you're visualizing, accentuate it and bring out that experience in your mind. Try to *feel* the color if you can.

Order. Creating a sequence of events or stories allows our brains to follow a visual pattern that helps us to remember. Creating these patterns and sequences not only builds creativity, it also assists us in grouping things and storing them safely in our brain. This is where techniques such as the Method of Loci help us connect random objects together (Chapter 3).

Positive Images. Happy, positive images make you feel all cozy inside and they do help you remember. Negative images are often as memorable or even more so. When visualizing you can use either: the bright red tomato looked so tasty I ate it; the tomato was rotten, but I still ate it—and then I vomited. The brain loves drama and gets attached to it.

Exaggeration. Make things much larger than they are in real life so your mind creates an extraordinary image to remember. Visualize a kebab six feet tall waddling down the road with garlic sauce dripping down its sides and crowds of screaming, hungry people running up to it, tripping over themselves from all directions with absolute joy. Unforgettable!

How It Works

Think of a subject and then apply SMASHIN' SCOPE to make it more memorable.

A Cat

In milliseconds you just visualized a cat. To make the cat more memorable we could color the cat red (Color), make it smell like it had farted (Senses), and have it jump up on top of you (Movement) to rub that smell on you (Senses). This (hopefully) is not a real-life scenario, so in its creation we used imagination, association with the cat and yourself, as well as exaggeration of the narrative. Try not to use your everyday logic when creating stories. Use your imagination to make silly, creative stories that will stick in your mind. After all, you are trying to make it memorable!

Make memorable stories from the following pairs of words using SMASHIN' SCOPE. Each pair has been divided into examples of concrete nouns, concrete + abstract nouns, and finally both abstract nouns. Concrete nouns already give us a visual of the word, but abstract nouns don't. You'll need to create an image for the abstract noun and connect it back to the other word.

cow + strike

....

toothpaste + hibernation

....

experience + mediation

....

SMASHIN' SCOPE helps integrate the logical part of your brain with the creative to enhance your mental capabilities. It may seem ridiculous to make things humorous or to use different colors, but you're still learning. The more you do these sorts of exercises in your head the more you'll discover what a practical difference they make in the real world. In meetings where you need to solve problems quickly, instead of having one or two ideas, you might now come up with five. Even in sports, instead of having three options to choose from, your mind can now think laterally and consider other scenarios. Often the best people in sports and business are creative and decisive. This does not have to be an innate thing. It can be learned by using simple tools such as SMASHIN' SCOPE.

How long? Once you've done some practicing it should take around thirty seconds to create a story using SMASHIN' SCOPE. For difficult, nonconcrete words, it may take up to one minute.

The Yellow Elephant Memory Model

My first book was called *The Yellow Elephant*, which also happens to be the name of a memory model I developed. It helps us to solve memory-related problems by following a four-step guide to make something memorable.

1. Abstract

Information, ideas, or concepts (without physical form), or things that do not make sense to us are likely to be abstract. This includes languages that we're unfamiliar with and highly specialized forms of learning such as quantum physics. Strings of numbers, words, and even people's names can be abstract. Abstract things are slippery to understand and don't mean anything to us unless an image is created inside our brain.

2. Image

To make things more memorable we need to convert the abstract into an image. We may or may not be able to understand what this abstract thing means, but by making it an image we prepare our mind to understand how to use it at step 3. The word "creativity," for example, is abstract, as it does not conjure up a specific image in our mind. If, however, we use the image of a light bulb or even that of Albert Einstein then we have converted the abstract nature of the word to an image we both recognize and understand.

3. Association

To complete the memorization process, we need a story connecting the elements through association. A strong association is made when what you're memorizing is physically connected. Earlier I used the example of pen and paper and how when the pen writes on paper, or better yet shreds the paper by pressing too firmly on it, a stronger association is made. The stronger the association, the more memorable it is.

4. Communication

How do you then make this memorable for others? Steps 1–3 occur in our own heads but communicating this to others may require some adapting and adjusting. What we create for ourselves may not suit or be appropriate for our audience, so we need to consider new ways to craft information that others can understand, whether it's study notes from class or grand public presentations.

How It Works

Remembering Names

Names are easy to forget because they are abstract in nature. There is no image for our brains to connect and store. So the trick to remembering names is to create the image and make an association.

If you're trying to remember the name Clare, for example, you could picture Clare being eaten by a bear. "Bear" will trigger the name Clare because they rhyme. You may also picture Clare looking like a bear. Or perhaps Clare has lots of hair sprouting from her nose, or claw-like hands! Make this image as graphic as you can. You may even imagine Clare being chased by a bear—but because there is no physical connection or contact between Clare and the bear it weakens the memorization. So even though there may be an emotional connection to the image, such as Clare's fear of the bear, a physical connection with your images will help you remember better.

When Listening

Words are extremely powerful and can have deep emotional connections—but only if they're visualized. You can listen to instructions, presentations, or even a friend chatting to you, but if you don't convert what you hear into images you may miss the importance of the message and increase your likelihood of forgetting. When listening to anything, visualize the images using SMASHIN' SCOPE principles to make better stories and you'll remember much more than before.

When Trying to Learn Anything New

When you first come across information it needs to be organized and arranged in a way for your brain to make sense of it and create images. Techniques such as mind mapping (Chapter 3) and drawings help you visualize and order information. Once you have visual order, you can make connecting stories.

KEY POINTS

- Imagination is the key to making anything more memorable.
- Build on foundation memory principles with SMASHIN' SCOPE and bring your story to life. You can practice on anything you can visualize.
- The Yellow Elephant Memory Model will help you when you are not sure how to remember something. Break it down by looking at how you can create memorable mental images and link the story.

CHAPTER 3

MEMORY TECHNIQUES

MANY PEOPLE BELIEVE having a great memory is a gift. When I was nineteen, I actually believed I had a "shocking" memory. I would forget names, directions, what I had just read, and even what people had said to me a minute ago. It was embarrassing; however, I accepted that I had not been born with a great memory—that is, until I stumbled upon memory techniques.

These "mental activities" made me use my imagination and little did I know how easy it was to improve my memory. Not only that, but I would go on to learn much faster, achieve more, and gain significant confidence in myself to do anything as I got older. Now it is your turn to experience the power of memory techniques.

Linking and Association

Linking and association is a technique that helps us remember effectively by creating stories using the items we want to remember in a sequential order. It's possible to link and associate any piece of information with another. Many people are unsuccessful in their early attempts to do this, though, because their links and connections are broken along the way to memorization.

How It Works

Let's say we had five items to remember. The linking process would look like this:

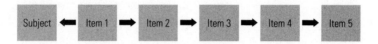

The first item is connected to the initial subject, and to the second item. Each subsequent item is connected to the one following it in a sequence.

How to Use

Remembering a list of words:

1. shoes
2. milk
3. mail carrier
4. donkey
5. blue

Imagine your **shoes** smelling profusely. You decide to take them off, and as you do **milk** starts to pour out! The milk splatters everywhere and somehow splashes into the eye of the

mail carrier. The mail carrier is angry, jumps on his **donkey** and starts to chase you. You run for your life and feel yourself getting sick and suddenly you turn **blue**!

To-do list:
1. Take out the garbage.
2. Buy the newspaper.
3. Pick up dry cleaning.
4. Work out at the gym.
5. Water the plants.

You head out of the house and suddenly the **garbage** can flips over and tips itself on top of you. The garbage is full of **newspapers** that stink like something has died in them. Before you retch, you head over to the **dry cleaners** to change into clean clothes. You feel refreshed and pumped, so much so that you're inspired to **work out at the gym**. You drink too much water during your workout and the toilets are out of order so you end up **watering the plants**.

With linking and association the word you are memorizing does not have to be exactly the same as how you memorize it. So if I try to remember the word "kaleidoscope," I might visualize and come up with something that sounds like the first part of the word, such as "calendar," where "cal" acts as a trigger to "kaleidoscope." My associative story could then be that I looked at my calendar and it was spiraling visually like broken mirrors.

How long? As long as it takes to read the paragraph and connect with the listed words, around one minute.

This book uses many triggers to form associations with words. Since we are using our own imagination everyone's stories and triggers will be different, so feel free to create your own triggers to the exercises in this book.

Number Rhyme
This is where the numbers rhyme with the words.

How It Works

one = gun   six = sticks
two = shoe   seven = heaven
three = tree   eight = gate
four = door   nine = wine
five = hive   ten = pen

How to Use
Let's say we want to remember the words on the right of the rhyming words. We link the rhyming list with the words-to-be-remembered list.

1. gun: elephant   6. sticks: water
2. shoe: breakfast   7. heaven: towel
3. tree: CD   8. gate: chocolate
4. door: computer   9. wine: tomato
5. hive: TV remote   10. pen: phone

The **elephant** is shot with a **gun**. (Luckily it does not die.)

You eat **breakfast** with your **shoe** as a spoon.

The **tree** outside is growing **CDs**.

The **door** opens onto a super**computer**.

There is a bee**hive** inside the **TV remote**.

You throw **sticks** into the **water** because you are bored.

As soon as you enter **heaven** you are given a refresher **towel**.

The **gate** is made out of **chocolate** and you have to bite your way through to enter.

You shove a whole **tomato** inside a **wine** bottle.

You draw smiley faces with your colored **pen** on a stranger's mobile **phone**.

Recall

All that's left now is to remember what happened with each of the rhyming numbers to give you the item you had memorized.

1. gun ....
2. shoe ....
3. tree ....
4. door ....
5. hive ....

6. sticks ....
7. heaven ....
8. gate ....
9. wine ....
10. pen ....

How long? Around ten seconds for each story from the previous examples, so a little under two minutes.

Number Shape

This is just like the number rhyme system but it uses images that look like the number instead of rhyming with it.

How It Works

one =

two =

three =

four =

five =

six =

seven =

eight =

nine =

ten =

How to Use

Let's say we want to remember the words on the right of the number shape words. We link the shape list with the words-to-be-remembered list.

1. candlestick	elephant	6. elephant's trunk	water
2. swan	breakfast	7. feathers	towel
3. trident	CD	8. glasses	chocolate
4. boat	computer	9. snake	tomato
5. hook	TV remote	10. bat and ball	phone

The **candlestick** burns the butt of the **elephant**.

The **swan** eats poached eggs for **breakfast**.

At **Trident** Motors they are giving away free One Direction **CDs**.

Your **boat** has a **computer** attached to the end of it for GPS navigation.

You grab your **TV remote** with a **hook** because you just can't be bothered getting up.

The **elephant's trunk** sprays **water** all over you at the zoo.

As the swan's **feathers** brush against you, you suddenly notice you are only wearing a **towel**.

Your **glasses** are drenched in **chocolate**. (Mmmm, chocolate.)

You feed your pet **snake** a juicy red **tomato**.

You hit the **ball with the bat** so hard that it breaks your neighbor's mobile **phone** as she is using it.

Recall

All that's left now is to remember what happened with each of the number shape words to give you the item you memorized.

1. candlestick	....	6. elephant's trunk	....
2. swan	....	7. feathers	....
3. trident	....	8. glasses	....
4. boat	....	9. snake	....
5. hook	....	10. bat and ball	....

How long? Around ten seconds for each story from the previous examples, so a little under two minutes.

Method of Loci

This memory technique creates locations and/or objects in a sequential order to store information. The storage is done through linking and association of the location and item to be memorized. The most important feature of this method is to remember information in sequence. The number of locations is almost limitless and I have over 300 sequential locations just while walking down the street!

How It Works
Here is a set of locations that might be a sequence.
1. front door
2. bed
3. shower
4. sink
5. cupboard

How to Use

Location	Item to be memorized
1. front door	mobile phone
2. bed	yogurt
3. shower	cucumber
4. sink	chainsaw
5. cupboard	tiger

You head toward the **front door** of your house and it turns into a huge **mobile phone**, which you have to swipe through to get inside. You hop into **bed** and you feel something sticky. Oh dear, someone has smothered **yogurt** all over the bed. You jump into the **shower** and rub **cucumber** all over your body thinking it is soap. You turn the **sink** tap on and it makes a buzzing **chainsaw** noise. You peer deeper into the sink and find a miniature chainsaw inside. You open the **cupboard** to find a live **tiger** all squashed inside, ready to jump out and attack.

Recall

All that's left to do now is to remember what happened in each of the locations to give you the item you memorized.

1. front door ....
2. bed ....
3. shower ....
4. sink ....
5. cupboard ....

How long? Around twenty seconds for each story from the previous examples, so a little under two minutes.

Mind Mapping

Mind mapping helps you organize information and ideas in a nonlinear manner. Mind Maps inventor, Tony Buzan, calls it a thinking tool that reflects externally what goes on inside your head. Often when we're thinking, things are not exactly organized. Thoughts are scattered and we need to gather together snippets of information from many places in our brain to understand something. A mind map allows you to create a complete plan all on one page so you can see direct and tangential links for specific topics. Mind maps can be used to make and take study notes, memorize books and even organize weddings! It is also a powerful technique for improved productivity, as demonstrated by the abundance of apps and software available, such as iMindMap, XMind, MindNode, MindGenius, NovaMind, and MindManager. But it's not necessary to buy software as they're easy to draw by hand.

How It Works

1. Take the main topic and put it at the center of a page.
2. Create section headings like thick branches starting at one o'clock and moving clockwise.
3. Create subheadings from the section headings.
4. Use color and images throughout to engage the brain.

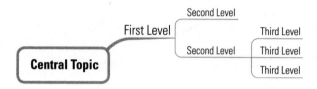

SWOT Analysis

This mind map has subheadings that create an order of information understood at a glance.

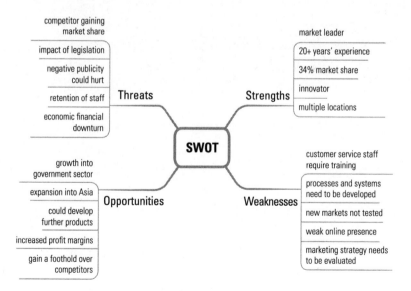

Speech Preparation

This next mind map is a forty-minute presentation I gave on two topics: the perfect job interview and time management. I also added time estimates to help me prepare more accurately. A mind map can be a great help with visual presentations if you're using software programs such as MS PowerPoint or Keynote.

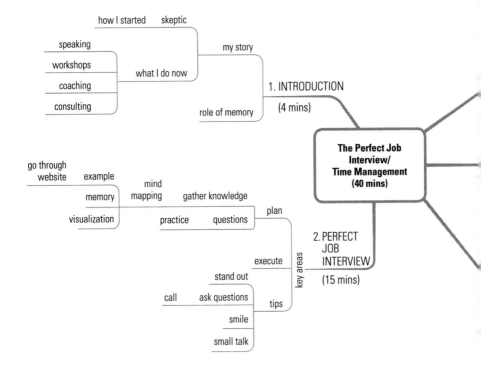

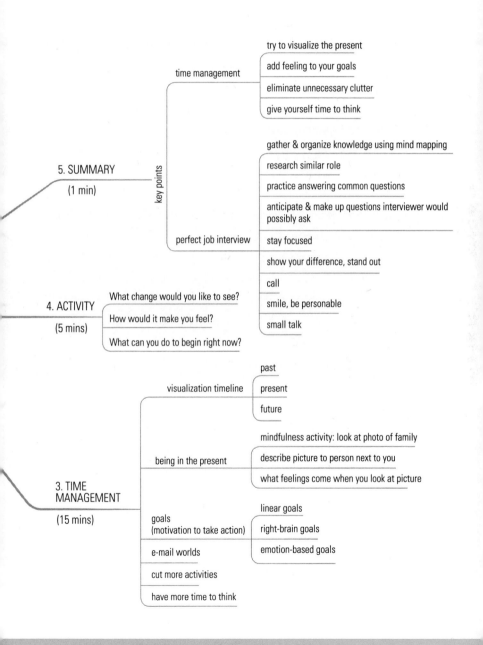

5. SUMMARY
(1 min)

key points

time management
- try to visualize the present
- add feeling to your goals
- eliminate unnecessary clutter
- give yourself time to think

perfect job interview
- gather & organize knowledge using mind mapping
- research similar role
- practice answering common questions
- anticipate & make up questions interviewer would possibly ask
- stay focused
- show your difference, stand out
- call
- smile, be personable
- small talk

4. ACTIVITY
(5 mins)
- What change would you like to see?
- How would it make you feel?
- What can you do to begin right now?

3. TIME MANAGEMENT
(15 mins)

visualization timeline
- past
- present
- future

being in the present
- mindfulness activity: look at photo of family
- describe picture to person next to you
- what feelings come when you look at picture

goals (motivation to take action)
- linear goals
- right-brain goals
- emotion-based goals

e-mail worlds

cut more activities

have more time to think

Speed-Reading

Imagine completing your reading in hours instead of weeks. Imagine, too, managing your social media and all those e-mails, reports, assignments, and documents with time to spare and a greater understanding of their content. Speed-reading truly can be life-changing, and for those who are not natural readers (like me) it can be especially rewarding. Bibliophobia is the fear of books and speed-reading cures that fear.

When we were children we were taught to read word by word. This is fine for learning how to read, but as your brain gets better at comprehending basic text you should be able to absorb information in larger chunks rather than individual words. Speed-reading uses techniques to encode words into images, enabling faster, more effective reading. Your brain has the ability to group together phrases so that you visualize what's happening rather than reading word by word. Speed-reading enables you to absorb information in chunks as you read; it creates better comprehension as you visualize groups of words together in context rather than each word.

How It Works: Using a Visual Guide

Reading with a finger or some sort of pointing device like a pen along the line helps to reduce the number of times you need to go back to reread. This in turn allows quicker reading.

How to Use a Visual Guide

Run your finger underneath the words as you read as a guide. This tricks your brain into reading more as your eyes will not only follow your guide, but see further along from the guide, forcing you to read faster. The more you practice, the less you'll notice your guide because you'll be so involved in the text. The more you're involved, the more you will remember. The more you remember, the better you will comprehend what you read.

How It Works: Using the Image Flow

Words are grouped into contextual meanings instead of set chunks. This results in a more consistent and visual flow of reading.

(The quick brown fox) (jumps over) (the lazy dog).

Words are grouped into their meaningful context. This enables the brain to process three phrases rather than reading nine individual words. If one word takes one second to read, then nine words will take nine seconds. But reading three phrases using image flow should take only a second to process each context, which means you will already be reading three times faster.

How to Use the Image Flow

Here is an exercise on how to view images in chunks using image flow. Try visualizing the content in brackets before moving along to the next bracket.

(Seven Tips) (to Reduce Stress at Work)

(In 2014) (I presented in Iran) (at the International Conference on Memory) (and Stress Management). (Here are seven tips) (on how to reduce stress) (and become a happier worker).

1. (Be aware)

(Most people are oblivious) (to the fact that they are stressed). (Their breathing changes), (heart rate increases) (and even their speech) (is faster than normal). (They can sometimes be a nuisance) (to others without even knowing). (Making a conscious effort) (to take a critical look) (at yourself) (and see if you're stressed) (can help you enormously). (Once you know you're stressed) (you are then able to) (take action) (to reduce that stress).

2. (Take a break)

(Often when stuck) (in front of the computer) (for hours) (things can get quite stressful), (especially if you're on a deadline). (Taking a quick power nap) (or a brisk) (fifteen-minute walk) (from a stressful situation) (can alleviate some stress symptoms).

3. (Be healthy)

(If all we're eating is rubbish), (then we will feel like rubbish). (Eating good food), (exercising), (and avoiding drugs) (all help to reduce stress). (One cool trick I've learned) (from Tony Buzan's book) (*Head Strong*) (is to keep telling yourself) (that "you are in the process) (of becoming healthy"). (This engages the brain) (in the present) (and helps you to) (take action). (Try it!)

4. (Have a laugh)

(A proven stress destroyer), (laughter can take your mind) (off things causing you stress) (stressors). (Watch some videos), (talk to some funny friends), (crack some jokes), (do whatever it takes) (to give yourself) (a positive experience) (so that you not only) (reduce stress), (but also enjoy life).

5. (Learn to say no)

(Here's a big one). (A lot of stresspots I've met) (in office environments) (have made a habit) (of saying yes) (to everything). (Stop it, dammit!) (Now!) (It creates further work), (pushes mental) (and physical boundaries), (and of course), (gives you more stress!) (You will also find) (that saying "no") (is so liberating). (Know when to say no) (and you will be) (saving yourself).

6. (Socialize)

(I know) (when I was stressed) (the last thing I ever wanted) (to do was meet up) (with people). (But research shows) (that socializing) (is a great form) (of reducing stress). (It takes you away) (from your bubble of life) (into the lives of others). (Suddenly you find yourself) (enjoying company) (and talking about things) (that are exciting) (and interesting), (again taking you away) (from worrying).

7. (Get rid of distractions)

(You wake up) (and first thing in the morning) (you check your e-mails). (You end up regretting it) (and it affects your mood) (while you're getting ready), (eating breakfast), (and traveling to work). (As soon as you get to work) (you switch your computer on) (and look at more e-mails). (Aghhh!) (They keep coming throughout the day) (and you just keep checking them). (What a life). (When you check your e-mail) (it creates a world in your head) (full of the content) (in the e-mail). (Some worlds are small), (some are massive), (some irrelevant). (In any case), (there are hundreds of worlds) (out there in your head) (that you are worrying about). (The best plan) (is to clear your head) (of these stories) (by checking your e-mail) (less often) (and doing them in "batches"), (as Timothy Ferriss explains) (in his book) (*The 4-Hour Workweek*). (This will help restore) (sanity into your life).

Practice speed-reading with a variety of materials to help you build your visual reading skills. It is not the easiest of memory techniques, but it may prove to be the most rewarding.

KEY POINTS

- Make sure your linking and association connections are not overlapping. Item 1 has no relationship with item 3, and while it may feel natural to assume a connection there, it could make you lose the order of memorization.
- Visualize your locations and objects in the Method of Loci as much as you can. Having imaginative and visually clear loci is a huge help with recall and retention in long-term memory.
- Mind maps order your information visually.
- When reading, use your finger as a guide by running it under the words. Doing this will not only help you read faster but also improve your comprehension.

CHAPTER 4

ADVANCED MEMORY TECHNIQUES

REMEMBERING NUMBERS CAN be really tricky unless you use a particular technique. Here are several that are incredibly useful.

The Major System

This encodes numbers into phonetic sounds based on the letters of the alphabet—but not vowels (including the letter *y*). The following numbers represent the letters next to it.

0 = s, z, c (ceiling)

1 = t or d

2 = n, gn

3 = m

4 = r

5 = l

6 = sh, j, dg (hedge), ch (chair), g (George)

7 = c, k, ck, ch (chord), g (goat)

8 = f, v, ph, gh

9 = p or b

How It Works

Take a pair of digits and make a few small words using the previous code. The number 32 can be man, for example, 77 cake, 86 fish, and 09 soap.

How to Use

There are many uses for the Major System, but it's mostly used for remembering a long series of numbers. (NB: You do not need to know the Major System codes by heart. Just have them close by for reference.)

Memorizing Numbers

To remember this twenty-digit number using the Major System, pair up the numbers and then make a story using linking and association.

92573391144768217282

92 (pen) + 57 (leg) + 33 (mummy) + 91 (bat) + 14 (door) + 47 (rock) + 68 (chef) + 21 (net) + 72 (gun) + 82 (fan)

> The **pen** writes a large squiggle on my **leg**. When I stand up I see a **mummy** three meters tall holding a **bat**. I run as fast as I can, open a **door** and go inside. There he is—the **Rock** holding eggs, about to bake a cake. He is dressed as a **chef**, wearing a **net** on his head. Then he swaps his net for a large machine **gun**, and his **fan**s watching applaud the action hero.

How long? Around two minutes to remember all the digits after reading the story.

Memorizing Playing Cards

Create an image for each card using the Major System or use these references.

Number	Spades	Clubs	Hearts	Diamonds
1 = t or d	A = seat	A = cat	A = hat	A = date
2 = n	2 = Sun	2 = cone	2 = hen	2 = den
3 = m	3 = sumo	3 = cam	3 = ham	3 = dam
4 = r	4 = sir	4 = car	4 = hair	4 = deer
5 = l	5 = sail	5 = coal	5 = hail	5 = doll
6 = sh, ch, j, dg	6 = sash	6 = cash	6 = hash	6 = DJ
7 = k, g, c, ck	7 = sack	7 = cake	7 = hook	7 = duck
8 = f or v	8 = safe	8 = coffee	8 = hoof	8 = dove
9 = p or b	9 = soap	9 = cap	9 = hoop	9 = tape
10 = s, z	10 = sauce	10 = case	10 = hose	10 = toes
11 = dd, tt, dt, td	J = sated	J = gutted	J = hated	J = dated
12 = tn, dn	Q = Satan	Q = kitten	Q = heathen	Q = titan
13 = tm, dm	K = spade	K = club	K = heart	K = diamond

The Method of Loci Revisited

Memorizing Numbers

Try the Method of Loci to store numbers in pairs for each location.

1.	front door	pen	Someone scribbled on the front door with a red pen.
2.	bed	leg	A leg was sticking out as I sat on my bed.
3.	shower	mummy	You opened the shower curtain to a large, scary mummy.

4.	sink	bat	The sink wasn't working so you hit it with a bat.
5.	cupboard	door	You opened the cupboard and found a secret door inside.
6.	television	rock	You watched the Rock wrestling on TV.
7.	couch	chef	The chef was cooking some food on your couch.
8.	dishwasher	net	You covered the dishwasher with a net.
9.	fridge	gun	You shot the fridge door handle with a gun to open it.
10.	table	fan	The fan was spinning so fast it sliced through the table.

Now recall the story from each location, which will in turn give you the word associated with the numbers.

1. front door ....
2. bed ....
3. shower ....
4. sink ....
5. cupboard ....

6. television ....
7. couch ....
8. dishwasher ....
9. fridge ....
10. table ....

How long? It will take ten to twenty seconds to make the story (connection) with a location and item to be memorized. So for ten items it's around three minutes.

Memorizing Playing Cards

Using the Method of Loci here's how to memorize ten random playing cards. Each card is connected to a location for an imaginative story to be made.

1.	front door	AS	Someone throws a seat at the front door.
2.	bed	7C	Your birthday cake is sitting on your bed.
3.	shower	9H	You hang up your shower curtain using metal hoops.
4.	bathroom sink	KD	The sink isn't working so you hit it with a diamond.
5.	cupboard	5D	You open the cupboard and find an old doll.
6.	television	10S	You clean the television with tomato sauce.
7.	couch	4H	There is dog hair all over your couch.
8.	kitchen sink	QC	You cover the kitchen sink with a fairly large kitten.
9.	fridge	3S	You try to protect your fridge from the sumo wrestler but fail.
10.	table	AC	The cat is dancing on the table.

After you've memorized ten playing cards, try doubling that effort to twenty. Ultimately your goal is to memorize fifty-two playing cards in fifty-two locations.

How long? It should take around twenty seconds to create a story with the location and card, so for the ten items it's around three minutes.

The Dominic System

Created by Dominic O'Brien, World Memory Champion for a record eight times, this technique is similar to the Major System and encodes digits into people and actions. The numbers coded are:

0 = O	5 = E
1 = A	6 = S
2 = B	7 = G
3 = C	8 = H
4 = D	9 = N

How It Works

Group the digits of numbers to be memorized into pairs. The letters of the first pair of digits creates a person using the initials of her first name and surname. The next pair relates to an action or activity of the person.

How to Use

Let's memorize this number using the Dominic System.

92593300154268217282

Number	Initial	First Name	Surname	Action
92	NB	Napoleon	Bonaparte	Fighting in battle
59	EN	Edward	Norton	Acting onstage
33	CC	Charlie	Chaplin	Putting on a large hat
00	OO	Ozzy	Osbourne	Screaming his lungs out
15	AE	Albert	Einstein	Writing equations on a blackboard
42	DB	Drew	Barrymore	Playing with her dog
68	SH	Stephen	Hawking	Speaking on his machine
21	BA	Ben	Affleck	Combing his hair
72	GB	George	Bush	Reading a book upside down
82	HB	Humphrey	Bogart	Posing

Using the table, we see that number 92 makes NB with $9 = N$ and $B = 2$. From this we can use the initials to create a name. In this case, **N**apoleon **B**onaparte. Since we have a person for the number 92, we can now attribute an action. In this case we have chosen Napoleon Bonaparte fighting in battle. The action element comes in when we are combining numbers together.

- The first two digits are always a person.
- The next two digits are always an action.

Using the Method of Loci to help, you can now use the person/action strategy of the Dominic System:

	Location	Numbers	Associative Story
1.	Front door	92 59	Napoleon Bonaparte acting onstage at your front door
2.	Bed	33 00	Charlie Chaplin screaming his lungs out on your bed
3.	Shower	15 42	Albert Einstein playing with his dog in the shower
4.	Bathroom sink	68 21	Stephen Hawking combing his hair in the bathroom sink
5.	Cupboard	72 82	George Bush posing in your cupboard

KEY POINTS

- You do not need to know the Major System codes as you start memorizing, just have them close by as a reference. Before long you'll know them by heart.
- When linking numbers make sure you don't mix up the order of the numbers you are trying to remember. If you make an incorrect story you will recall incorrect numbers.
- When using the Method of Loci to remember numbers, always attach the story deeply into the location. Remember, physical connection makes for stronger memorization.
- The Method of Loci is the fastest way to memorize playing cards. Create as many loci as you can so you don't get your stories mixed up by repeatedly using the same location.
- Creating a spreadsheet listing people and their actions is super helpful when using the Dominic System.
- Impress others with these new skills and spread the love.

CHAPTER 5

PLAN, THEN ACT

*"The great aim of education is not knowledge
but action."*—Herbert Spencer

SO NOW YOU'RE completely across the principles and techniques of memory training. In the following chapters you'll see how to apply them to many different topics and will soon be able to apply them to *any* area of learning you want. In my thirteen years as a memory trainer I haven't met anyone—from the ages of four to over ninety—who wasn't able to use these strategies.

Anyone who has an imagination is able to use memory techniques to enhance their memory.

Ah, I hear you saying, it's not that simple. Sure, it requires commitment, but if you want to learn more about the world and the millions of wonderful things in it (and out of it) then stick with it for a while. Too often we give up on things before we really get started. New Year's resolutions are a perfect example of this. Don't wait til January 1 to try new things, but do take some time to plan a strategy and mark your time carefully.

Common Roadblocks to Success

There is more than one reason why people fail to achieve their goals.

A Lack of Discipline

According to self-development entrepreneur Brian Tracy, discipline is being able to do what you need to do, when you need to do it, whether or not you like it. Get into the headspace of working toward your goals even at difficult times. Such sacrifices mean not just achieving your resolution, but creating a successful habit.

A Lack of Passion

On New Year's Day (depending on if you're nursing a hangover) anything seems possible. But as the weeks roll on other things happen and what motivation you had is compromised. Before embarking on a new project, create an image of your goal in your head. Write it down. Then hit it with all the feelings that achieving it will give you. If you want to learn a new language or skill, say, visualize how great it would be to speak that language. Write down all the feelings that it will give you and keep adding to it. How would you feel speaking the language when traveling, or for work? The more emotion and feeling you have, the fiercer your pursuit of the goal will be.

A Lack of Focus

Your goals end up being "too hard." You've managed initial steps then realized that it's going to take much more energy and effort. At this point you start to feel overwhelmed and you give up. Instead, create a plan with all the steps necessary to complete your goal. Knowing what's needed makes the journey easier.

A Lack of Accountability

Being accountable for your actions increases the chances of reaching your goals. It's easier, too, if there are other people, friends or family, who share the same goal. Search around. If not, are there any clubs or societies you can join? You can let yourself down, but letting others down is much more disappointing.

Too Busy

People often tell me they "don't have the time" to do what they want to, and it's true we're busy—possibly working several jobs, looking after children and maybe elderly parents. Plan each day the night before and rid yourself of time-wasting distractions. Practice the Pomodoro Technique—breaking down tasks into twenty-five-minute intervals with a couple of minutes' break in between—for better time management and you'll be surprised. Then work on your goals.

Too Forgetful

Learning memory techniques is not just about remembering, it's also about creating successful habits of the mind. Visualization is the key to memory. So try to use your imagination for everything!

Caught Up in Negative Thoughts

There may be people out there who do not want you to succeed, but if you start to worry about them then you will likely fail. Instead, focus on the passion you have for achieving this goal to sail through the negativity. It's not easy, but it is oh so rewarding once you get there.

Formula for Success

With coaching I get to provide people with knowledge and skills to make positive changes in their lives. Here's my coaching formula to help you succeed.

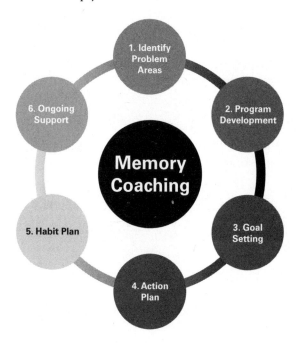

Identify Problem Areas

Make a comprehensive list of the things that are stopping you from learning as you'd like to. You may find that the only barriers are ones you've created in your mind. Or they could be physical, financial, time-based, skills-based, or geographical.

Program Development

Now list all the knowledge, skills, and resources you may need to fix the problems.

Problem Area	How Does It Feel?	Knowledge	Skills	Resources
Slow reading	Like I'm getting nowhere Not understanding what I read	How to read faster How to improve understanding	Speed-reading Memory techniques	Courses, books; coaching; find someone who reads better
Don't have the time to learn	Like I'm delaying something I should get on with Everyone else can, why not me?	How to manage time	Time management Memory	Share goals with family and friends to build accountability; use the Pomodoro Technique

After listing your problem areas complete your resources column because you may not have the information for the knowledge and skills columns until you've done a little research.

Goal Setting

In a similar table, list your goals—but this time instead of a "How does it feel?" column, have one titled "How will it feel?"

Goals	How Will It Feel?	Knowledge	Skills	Resources
To remember names easily	Great—confident about meeting people	How to remember names	Memory techniques	Get coaching; find people who are great at remembering names
To learn anything quickly	Empowering Better career prospects	How to learn faster and better	Learning strategies Memory techniques Mind mapping Speed-reading Self-discipline	Find all materials for faster learning, memory techniques, speed-reading, and mind mapping

The "feel" column provides a strong emotional response to the brain that stimulates further action to help you reach your goals quicker. Have a vision using emotion!

Action Plan

Start the work: read those books, attend those seminars, perhaps get a coach. Whatever it takes to achieve your goal, write it down. This will become your road map to success.

Habit Plan

You have a plan, but you need to create habits for your actions so that when working on your goals, the tasks come to you naturally. That's the point of creating a habit. You might have all the resources and plans at your fingertips, but unless you make it a habit you simply won't do the work.

Ongoing Support and Review

As you work toward your goals, make sure you have someone to check in with from time to time for encouragement and support. Don't try to go it alone.

Achieving Goals: How I Memorized the *Yellow Pages* in 24 Days

After nine long years of training, competing, and coaching through my business, I decided to quit memory training. It was one of the toughest decisions I had ever made because I just loved what I did, but study, health, and family issues needed to take priority at that time. Two weeks after this I received a phone call from a PR company that wanted me, as the Australian Memory Champion, to memorize the

Yellow Pages phone books as part of a marketing campaign for the brand.

My initial reaction was one of disbelief, but after discussions we worked out what I needed to memorize—more than 2,000 business names and their phone numbers. They gave me some time to think about it and days later I was sitting on the couch with my laptop about to write a "thanks, but no thanks" e-mail, knowing that this task would further add to the chaos that was my life at the time.

Then suddenly something clicked.

I knew I could memorize a phone book. I knew this was something I could do and I had to prove it to myself. I knew this opportunity had come about because of my hard work in the memory business for so many years, and to say no would have been like turning my back on that work. So I redid the calculations in my head: if it took thirty seconds to memorize one advertisement, then I should be able to manage 2,000 ads in around twenty days. If I went ahead with it, I would have to take time off work, miss some university classes, and, hardest of all, go without seeing my then two-year-old son for most of the day. Still, by being super organized and making slight sacrifices, I would achieve something no one else had. I retyped my e-mail—"I'll do it"—and pressed send.

The SMART (sensible, measurable, achievable, relevant, timely) goals that I learned in management class went out the window. In order to achieve something that had never been done before, I had to create a new plan.

To be honest, I didn't even think, "What if I can't remember?" or, "What if I get the numbers wrong?" Somehow I just knew I could do it. I believed in myself, and belief is such a powerful thing. I had twenty-four days before I would be tested in public at a convention and also give several live TV and radio interviews.

At last the A–K and L–Z volumes of Sydney's *Yellow Pages* arrived (they were much thicker than Melbourne's). I flicked through the pages and thought about the best strategy to memorize this beast. I needed to ensure I had enough time to test myself and revise, and to have confidently memorized 20,000-plus digits that made up the businesses.

I used SMASHIN' SCOPE to picture the name of each business. This was critical. If I didn't have a strong image for each business, then it would be almost impossible to recall its numbers. Then I memorized the numbers using the Major System, decoding phonetic sounds for numbers. So the process was to visualize the advertisement and then link the number of the business to my visualization. To remember the ad for Bob's Cleaning 9217 7747, for example, I first imagined a person bobbing down and scrubbing the floor as hard as he could. Then I linked it to the number by having cleaner Bob take out his "pen" (92), write his invoice on his "dog" (17) with the dog jumping into a "cake" (77). As the dog jumped into the cake, "Rocky Balboa" (47) jumped up yelling "Adriaaaaaaan."

It took a good thirty seconds to do this for each ad. For all you memorizers out there, there were many reasons I did not use the Method of Loci. Firstly, it would have taken longer and I couldn't have memorized the ads in the time I had. Secondly, I didn't have enough locations. Thirdly, as I was going to be tested at *random*, there was no point trying to remember the order, which is the Method of Loci's specialty. Instead, I chose the basic linking strategy and it worked exactly how I wanted it to.

I had also learned from a rookie mistake I made some time earlier on 1116 SEN radio when interviewed by Billy Brownless, Tim Watson, and Andy Maher. They got me on the show to talk about memory and gave me a short memory test of ten words. I assumed it would be easy because we memorizers remember hundreds of words in single sittings. I had even picked my favorite location to use. (The Method of Loci is popular with memorizers in competition and one of the most powerful memory techniques there is.) I thought I had it covered. Boy, was I wrong! Of the ten items they tested me on, I only remembered three! Listeners called up the station saying I was a fake and that they had memorized more than I had. The presenters also had a good laugh at my expense. From this I learned that you might know sensational memory techniques but if you don't use the right one for the right occasion you'll end up with egg on your face.

That first night of memorization was very nearly the last. I had memorized for seventy minutes but only got through fifty ads. My wife tested me but the results were disappointing. I didn't know if I should continue, and I had barely even started.

I was in this now though. I had to continue. Fortunately, work gave me two weeks off so I could focus fully on the task at hand. And I was very conscious of how important it was to remain healthy—to drink lots of fluids and eat right, remain positive, and pray like crazy!

The next day I did slightly better. The day after that, much better. Consistency was what I was looking for. Once I had gotten into a groove it was almost robotic. I was memorizing sixty ads in sixty minutes. Although it doesn't seem like much of an improvement from the first night, my recall was far better. I was memorizing sixty ads and going back three more times to rememorize them; I memorized sixty ads four times and then moved on to the next lot of sixty. I averaged around five hours a day memorizing. Some days I did slack off, but the following day I would put in a solid eight hours. The longest day was memorizing for ten hours, memorizing in five blocks of two hours with a break in between.

Earlier I wrote about the importance of accountability. What helped me get through this challenge was the fact that I tweeted my progress daily, which held me accountable to my followers and friends. My dedication surprised even me, because in memory competitions I rarely memorized for more than ten minutes in a sitting!

That final week my white office table had become yellow, stained from the phone books, and I had a yucky metallic taste in my mouth from turning thousands of pages. By day eighteen I had memorized both books. So I went back to revise the ads all over again to firm up my recall. I had six days to do this. Beginning again, I almost doubled my initial speed—120 ads per hour—with even better recall.

On arriving in Sydney I found myself swamped with television, radio, and media interviews. I was tested live on national television and radio, but this time the hard work, strategy, consistency, and sacrifices all paid off. I did make a couple of mistakes, it's true, but the client and the PR company were thrilled and it was regarded as a great success.

KEY POINTS

- List your goals: We've heard it before, but listing your goals in life can be an eye-opening experience. Writing them down makes them fully conscious, and your brain will love you for it. Put the list on your fridge or desk where you'll regularly see it. The more your goals are in the front of your mind the more progress you'll make.

- Remember to feel: Close your eyes and visualize how it would feel to achieve your goals. These feelings are the most important drivers you have. If you don't have an emotional connection to a goal then you're only looking at a set of tasks and to-do lists. Feelings put you in a mental state of accomplishment even before you've accomplished anything.

- Begin now: Not tomorrow. Not next week. Now! It could be as simple as picking up the phone and calling someone. Start acting now and you are one step closer to success.

USING THESE TECHNIQUES

"Time moves in one direction, memory in another."—William Gibson

DID YOU KNOW?

In 2015, the fourth most powerful supercomputer in the world took forty minutes to simulate just one second of human brain activity.

CHAPTER 6

EVERYDAY MEMORY

*"You never realize what a good memory you have
until you try to forget something."*—Franklin P. Jones

ACCORDING TO THE Alzheimer's Association, Alzheimer's is the sixth leading cause of death in the United States, and deaths attributed to the disease increased by 71 percent between 2000 and 2013. It is predicted that by 2050 nearly 13.8 million Americans will suffer from some sort of dementia, an alarming statistic particularly as there is no known cure for the disease at this time. It's little wonder then that people are becoming more and more conscious of brain health and want to exercise it every day.

We may not need to be memory champions, memorize books, learn languages in a month, or perform amazing memory feats, yet there are so many everyday things we do that are made so much easier by having a better memory.

Where Did I Leave My Keys?
A common problem around the world is remembering where we left our keys. It's astonishing that this is such a common

thing to forget and we've all done it at least once, but if you keep doing it maybe it's time to fix the problem. Try the following steps to help you always remember where you put your keys.

Visualize

Create a vivid image of where you put the keys to help with recall. Since this happens in your head, we can exaggerate to make that visualization really stand out. As you put your keys on the table imagine that the keys grow in size:

- Picture your keys getting bigger and bigger.
- Listen to the sound they make as they grow.

Associate

Linking the item to be remembered with another item allows for better recall. Once again, since it is happening in your mind, you can be creative and make that association stand out. As the keys grow to an extraordinary size the table breaks in half, unable to carry the weight of the keys:

- Imagine the keys becoming heavy enough to break the table.
- Picture the table breaking in half.
- Listen to the sound of the table breaking.

Recall

Recall can be either conscious or accidental.

Conscious: You remember the association with "keys breaking the table." Ah, *table*!

Accidental: You walk around your house looking for the keys and pass the table. You stop and ask yourself, "Why did the table break? Oh, the keys broke it." *Voila!*—You find the keys.

How to Remember Everything Before Leaving the House

As you're about to head out the front door, visualize and associate all that you need to take with you. If you need to take your keys, phone, phone charger, bag, and important contract documents for signing, individually link each item to the door. You need to visualize each story as you are about to head out the door.

1. As you are about to exit the front door a huge metallic **key** whacks you in the face.
2. Your **phone** is now the size of the door and as it rings it causes the front door to vibrate.
3. The **phone charger** is blocking your exit as you try to leave.
4. You trip backward over your **bag** as you try to head out of the door.
5. The front door is made of very thin paper and it needs to be signed, reminding you of the **contract**.

The front door is only a trigger to help you remember before you leave the house. Other triggers might include when you get into your car, or as you put on your shoes.

Remembering Where You Parked Your Car

We've all forgotten at least once where we've parked, but walking around and around busy multilevel parking garages can be frustrating and embarrassing. If you know how to memorize numbers you can memorize the level number if there is one.

If there isn't then find something in your surroundings as a visual connection. Perhaps you parked outside and there are trees about 100 yards away roughly at a one o'clock direction. You can make a story of how trees crashed onto your car at 1 P.M. The trick is to find something unique and associate it with your car—but do not involve any other car as it may not be there when you get back!

Remembering Shopping Lists

The simplest way to remember shopping lists is to use the memory techniques of linking and association. To remember the following list we need to create an imaginative story connecting one item to the other.

1. seltzer water
2. flour
3. raspberry
4. chocolate syrup
5. toilet paper
6. pineapple
7. cat food
8. dishwashing liquid
9. window cleaner
10. popcorn

You walk into the supermarket and you are sprayed with **seltzer water** by the staff. Just as you wipe yourself off, someone from the checkout accidently spills **flour** over you. Everyone is watching and you're embarrassed and turn red like a **raspberry**. Of course you know the best cure for embarrassment—a spoonful of **chocolate syrup** right down the hatch. But the syrup makes you nauseous. Your tummy starts grumbling and you run as fast as you can and dive into boxes of **toilet paper**. As you come up for air you feel a large **pineapple** ring around your neck. You take a bite and realize it's actually **cat food** you're eating. Now you feel sick again and need to wash your mouth out. You grab the **dishwashing liquid** and give your mouth a good clean. Your mouth is frothing and bubbles are going everywhere so you grab **window cleaner** off the shelf to spray the bubbles away. It works and you celebrate by treating yourself to your favorite **popcorn**.

If you need to memorize more than twenty items, it's best to use the Method of Loci, as your story will get very long and one weak link in the story chain means you could forget everything after the last item you remembered. If, however, you memorize a lot of items and prefer to use linking and association methods, make sure your story is highly visual, imaginative, and links physically to the next item.

Remembering Names

A good way to remember names is to visualize the person first. What's memorable about his appearance? Does he have a big nose? Long hair? Piercings? Exaggerate some feature even if he looks remarkably normal otherwise. By doing this, you create a strong holding spot for the information to be memorized—in this case the person's name.

This is Bruce.

To make him memorable, I picture him with a bald head, wearing colorful running shoes, pants, and a football T-shirt. Now that we have a memorable visual of the man, we need to create a separate visual for the name "Bruce." The first thing that comes to my mind is Bruce Lee, the martial arts movie star. I could also use another Bruce, I know, but Bruce Lee makes a more interesting story involving punches, spinning roundhouse kicks, and cries of "Hayaaaa!"

Now for the fun part—creating the story. Visualize the person with colorful running shoes, football T-shirt, and bald head being attacked by Bruce Lee himself yelling "Hayaaaa!" All that is left to do is to recall the name. Go back to the person you initially created an image for and think about what happened to him. In this example it was being attacked by Bruce Lee. As soon as you recall Bruce Lee, it will trigger the name Bruce.

These techniques are also helpful in remembering appointments, your kids' schedules, and running errands such as picking up the dry cleaning or dropping off shoes to be repaired.

Everyday Technology

Technology is great when it helps us live more productive, better lives, but it can also cause headaches. What we presume is making us more advanced could in fact be dragging us behind. Here are some ways to help deal with annoying everyday technology problems that help exercise our minds at the same time.

Passwords

We have so many logins these days it's difficult to remember them all, but we do know that using the same password repeatedly is neither secure nor smart. Even so, many websites demand a minimum of eight alphanumeric characters, including capital letters, and some workplaces insist you change your login each month! Memory techniques take the guesswork out of remembering multiple passwords.

What needs to be memorized:

- The password itself
- Username
- The website or service you are logging into

These three items need images that are interconnected. It's no use trying just to remember a password because you may not remember what to use the password for.

Let's say I want to remember an e-mail account login and have these details:

Username: damocraig@yahoo.com
Password: sMfxFgjQ
Website: Yahoo! Mail

Damo and Craig are my cats' names so I visualize them and connect them both to Yahoo! via association. I visualize my cats in the morning after they've been fed with their victory cry, "Yahooooo! We have eaten." (Believe me, if they could speak that's exactly what they'd say.) Next is the password, a jumble of letters in upper- and lowercase, currently abstract with no meaning to anyone. Using the Yellow Elephant Memory Model we can turn the abstract into images through storytelling:

A small snail (s) goes up a large mountain (M) and as he goes up hears some very strange faint sound effects (fx) coming from a huge fireplace (F) where someone has thrown tiny goji (gj) berries. As soon as the snail picks up the berries, the Queen (Q), who happens to be nine feet tall, walks in.

Notice how I visualized small and faint images for lower-case letters and large, bold things for uppercase? Remember this trick. Also, be sure you use SMASHIN' SCOPE to make your visualization stand out. All that is left to do is to connect Damo and Craig with the snail story and we have memorized our Yahoo! e-mail password. When recalling this information, the first thing we see is the site or service to enter our details, so we begin our story from that point:

> Damo and Craig cry "Yahoooo!" after breakfast when suddenly they realize they have eaten snails. One of the smaller snails escapes the food bowl and climbs up a large mountain (M) and hears some very strange faint sound effects (fx) coming from a huge fireplace (F) where someone has thrown tiny goji (gj) berries. As soon as the snail picks up the berries the Queen (Q), who happens to be nine feet tall, walks in.

It may seem like a lot of mental work just to remember one password. But you should only need to do it once. Once you've reviewed your story a few times you should be set.

Here are some passwords to memorize.

K4nmQq5Q
wBsUtpsr
j242PEPX
QybZJTnB
UCbXvfQD

Once you've got the hang of making up stories, converting from abstract to image, see if you can use something similar for your own passwords. You can generate random passwords by visiting *www.random.org/passwords*. You can create passwords this way, or you could play with a mixture of letters, words, and numbers that make sense to you. You can even join two different passwords together in upper- and lowercase.

Just make sure you don't use any of these, which are the twenty-five worst passwords: 123456; password; 12345; 12345678; qwerty; 1234567890; 1234; baseball; dragon; football; 1234567; monkey; letmein; abc123; 111111; mustang; access; shadow; master; michael; superman; 696969; 123123; batman; trustno1.

PINs

You probably have to memorize various PINs, which can be four or six digits long, for credit cards and ATM cards. The key elements to memorize here are:

- The service you are using for your PIN
- The PIN itself

Say, for example, I want to remember my PIN for general ATM use.

Bank card: ABC Bank
PIN: 677501

Create a visual for the ABC Bank and the number 677501 using the Major System or Dominic System to encode the numbers into images.

The Giants and Cardinals baseball teams both greet you as you walk toward the ATM. You're about to put your card into the machine and the Giants gives you a piece of chocolate

(67) while the Cardinals take your chocolate and glue (75) it to the ATM. As soon as it's glued, both the teams tell you to sit (01).

Credit Card Numbers

Credit cards require more than just memorizing numbers and the key elements to memorize are:

- The type of card
- The card number
- Expiration date
- Security code
- PIN

The type of card: VISA
The card number: 7833 2690 6563 1980 4323
Expiration date: 03/2019
Security code: 671
PIN: 1134

Create a visual for VISA, the card number, expiration date, security code, and PIN.

You arrive in a foreign country and unfortunately you do not have a VISA. You start coughing (78) to the mummy (33) next to you and receive a nudge (26) from the boss (90). You turn around to find that they have packed your luggage into a large shell (65) but they forgot the jam (63). You get annoyed so you gently tap (19) the face (80) of the ram (43) that was sitting quietly next to the garden gnome (23). The officer comes along and asks you when your card expires and you tell him your sumo (03) wrestler's nose (20) is dripping like a tap (19).

The officer gets confused then asks for your code. You tell him it's in your jacket (671). He reaches into your jacket and finds a piece of paper with a PIN, and the following words written on it: "Teddy (11) is being held hostage by Mary (34)."

Telephone Numbers

Key elements to memorize:

- The person/business/place
- The phone number

Let's say you want to remember your friend Bob's number.

Bob Sears
Ph: 0491779841

Create a visual for Bob Sears and the number 0491779841 using the Major System or Dominic System to encode the numbers into images.

A person is constantly bobbing up and down (Bob) in a Sears (Sears) shopping store among the electrical goods. Bob suddenly gets a baseball bat (91) and takes a swing at you, but he misses and whacks a cake (77) instead. You go to take a bite of it but it's made of beef (98) and there are rats (41) running out of it.

You can, of course, use the Method of Loci for storing longer numbers if you like. It's up to you how you memorize them, but as long as you create the story by encoding it will work.

Stress Management

Stress can take away our ability to progress in life and keep us stuck in a hole that we feel we cannot escape from. Using visualization, and especially through using SMASHIN' SCOPE, we can create relaxing stories that make us breathe a whole lot better.

> Imagine yourself on a beautiful island. The sun is up and the temperature is perfect. You get up from lying down on the soft sandy beach and make your way into the crystal clear water. You dip your right foot into the water and it gives you a tiny chill sensation, which rushes from your feet all the way to your brain. You slowly walk through the water, feeling how soft the sand is on the soles of your feet as the water moves between your toes.

You can either read the previous paragraph or feel it in your mind as an experience. Go back and reread it and this time visualize and feel what's happening. Hear the sounds around you, feel the warmth and the chill, let your mind wander.

Was it different the second time? Did you feel you were there? Being in the moment is a powerful strategy when dealing with stress. Using visualization techniques like this help you take a break from the real world and go to a place that soothes the mind.

Continue the story and make it longer, or think of another relaxing story. Will it involve nature, your family, success? Whatever it is use SMASHIN' SCOPE to bring your story to life. Close your eyes for even greater effect.

KEY POINTS

- The three-step process of remembering keys will also help you recall other daily things like taking the bins out, or whether you've fed the animals.
- Use the number systems for all number-based items or dates including phone numbers, PINs, credit cards— wedding anniversaries work well here too!
- Use your SMASHIN' SCOPE skills to create amazing visual stories for stress relief.

CHAPTER 7

STUDY TECHNIQUES

"The whole purpose of education is to turn mirrors into windows."—Sydney J. Harris

MOST OF US have spent our entire educational life learning through repetition. Indeed, most of the world still works this way, and probably will for some time yet. Many learners and educators might acknowledge other learning methods, but the safety and ease of rote learning ultimately triumphs. It's a proven system, right? It's produced so many academic champions and shaped learning culture around the world.

But there's still a problem.

Repetition sucks. It takes a long time and we often forget and are forced to repeat things over and over again. Today's students are given so much information that they don't have time to review material, so it's no surprise they end up forgetting it. Then when it's exam time they endure the ritual of overnight cramming—a bizarre practice that is also a widely accepted form of learning!

Personally, I was never a master of cramming. I couldn't bear the long hours and I'd get super stressed. My eyes were truly opened for the first time when I learned about memory techniques when still a student. Before that I had always assumed I had a bad memory. Learning memory techniques engaged the creative side of my brain, which I loved. I've always been imaginative but had never used my imagination for studying before because I learned by rote. Whole-brain learning, which incorporates memory techniques such as mind mapping, linking systems, and speed-reading, won me over in a big way. And I didn't stop there. I knew that if it could help me it would be fantastic for other students too.

How to Study Faster and Better

We often don't think about why we study; it's just something we do because we have to, usually as part of school or a university course. Becoming more conscious about how we learn, however, helps us understand ourselves better and makes us more self-aware. This self-awareness can spark a deeper interest around specific subjects, driving deeper engagement and bringing real meaning to our learning efforts.

What Do You Want to Get Out of Your Learning?

If you're at school, is your motivation to get top grades or is it to satisfy your parents? If you're already working, are you studying to get better at your job or to find a new one? This is all fine, but have you ever thought about what you really *want* to learn? You may be an accountant who wants to learn how to cook Asian food, or to play a musical instrument. Wanting to learn something helps your mind become more receptive to new information because you're more engaged with the subject matter.

How Will You Motivate Yourself to Study?

It's difficult to study something that's boring and dry. The trick is to change boring to exciting by using the Yellow Elephant Memory Model. Just imagine that the topic is the abstract, then create an image. Here you can use your visual skills, mind mapping, drawing, singing, dancing, or whatever you feel connects with the content you're reading. Try transforming multiple pages from a boring old textbook into a graphic representation on one page. With practice, you can turn something dry into something memorable.

Mathematics

I was never brilliant at math. I just scraped through at secondary school, and at university I failed it three times, making my undergraduate degree take years longer than it should have! After getting into all things memory and brain related, though, I understood that my difficulties with math came about because it really is another language, one that was not well communicated to me or well understood by me. What I have since found to be a real help with the building blocks of mathematics is to memorize formulas.

Memorizing Formulas

Shape Areas

We need to substitute images for symbols and letters to make stories that connect the logical sequence of the formula. For the multiplication symbol × we can have the action: jump. So now let's apply the stories.

Triangle

area = ½ × b × h

b = base

h = height

You walk **half**way up the triangle then realize you need to get down. You **jump** on its **base** and then immediately **jump** as **high** as you can to get to the top.

Rectangle

area = w × h

w = width

h = height

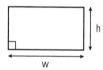

You roll across the **width** of the rectangle to find a huge spider millimeters away, which causes you to **jump** up to the **height** of the ceiling.

Ellipse

area = π × a × b

You are eating a **pie**, which looks like an ellipse. The sauce runs down your shirt and you **jump** up, yelling "**Aay!**" Suddenly you **jump** up a second time after a **bee** lands on you.

Trapezium
area = ½(a+b) × h
h = height

You walk **half**way up the trapezium and realize that you have to **jump** on top of both of your friends, "**Amy + Ben**." Embarrassed and ashamed, you step back and **jump** extremely **high**.

Parallelogram
area = b × h
b = base
h = height

You see something on the **base** of the parallelogram and move closer to investigate. It's a snake and you **jump** up as **high** as you can from fright!

Circle
area = π × r^2
r = radius

After eating your circular **pie** you **jump** on the **rollercoaster—twice**!

Trigonometry

θ = theta, which can equal
the action "dance/dancing"
/ = separating
sin = sign
cos = cos lettuce (a.k.a. romaine)
tan = Tanner
csc = casket
sec = secretary
cot = cot
opposite = opposite
hypotenuse = hippopotamus
adjacent = agent

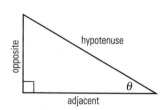

Formula: **sin θ = opposite/hypotenuse**

> You're holding a **sign** while **dancing**. **Opposite** you is a barrier **separating** you from the **hippopotamus**.

Formula: **cos θ = adjacent/hypotenuse**

> You are eating **cos lettuce** while **dancing**. An **agent** pops out of nowhere and tells you to **separate** yourself from the **hippopotamus**.

Formula: **tan θ = opposite/adjacent**

> **Tanner** is **dancing**. Directly **opposite** him is an **agent** who is disgusted. Luckily, there is a barrier **separating** them.

Formula: **csc θ = hypotenuse/opposite**

> The **casket** is being **danced on** by rowdy **hippopotamuses**. They must be **separated** and report to the **opposite** end of the room to be disciplined. Naughty hippos.

Formula: **sec θ = hypotenuse/adjacent**

The **secretary** is **dancing** on her desk. The rowdy **hippopotamus** is about to join in when suddenly he is **separated** by animal safety **agents**.

Formula: **cot θ = adjacent/opposite**

The **cot** has **dance** music blaring out of it from a speaker. The hotel manager calls in the **agents** to **separate** the speaker and put it at the **opposite** end of the room.

Algebra

Quadratic Formula

$$x = \frac{-b \pm \sqrt{b^2 - 4ac}}{2a}$$

= = extremely loud

x = xylophone

−b = blown away

± = clown

√ = heart

b² (squared) = one of the bananas in *Bananas in Pyjamas*, B2

− = takes away

4ac = 4 apples with multiple cinnamon doughnuts

———————— = divided by

2a = 2 apples

The **xylophone** is being played **extremely loudly** and is eventually **blown away** by an angry **clown**. Your **heart** starts racing, then one of the bananas in *Bananas in Pyjamas*, **B2**, comes to help. He **takes away** your fear by giving you **4 apples with multiple cinnamon doughnuts**. You are very kind and **divide 2** of the **apples** to share with friends.

How to Write a Good Essay

Studying is not just about gathering knowledge and making sense of it, though; it's also about showing that you understand that knowledge, and the most common way we do this is through written essays, reports, and exams. The real stumbling block to success in writing comes from not carefully organizing your thoughts and approach, so planning is essential. Our sample essay comes from Monash University's Language and Learning Online site.

Look Closely at the Essay Topic

Here's the assignment:

> In the last twenty years, rates of divorce have risen significantly in Western countries. Critically analyze some of the different explanations given for this phenomenon. In your discussion you should consider what implications these explanations might have for social policy.

Order the Information

The first thing to do is identify the topic, which here is **rates of divorce** (in Western countries). Now we need to establish a structure for the essay. Most are pretty straightforward, requiring an introduction, three or four main points (or paragraphs) in the body of the essay using quotes or references to support your argument, then a conclusion with a final point or recapping on points already made.

By analyzing the question we can create a mind map structure for our essay:

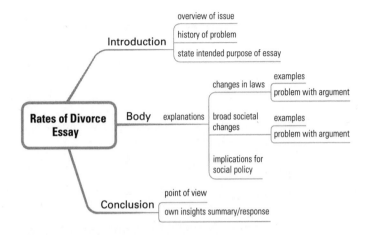

Write to Fill in the Structure

Once you've established the shape of the essay it's much easier to write the content to follow the different points that need to be made.

Fill in the Gaps

Once you create your branches you can clearly see what you need to write about. If you get stuck, simply move on to another branch and continue. It's not necessary for you to write chronologically, and because you've created the structure the pieces will all fit together. It's a little like having a skeleton—now you need to add flesh to it.

Include Supporting Material

- *Use Quotes:* Experts can help effectively support your argument succinctly.
- *Use Facts:* Facts help bolster your argument—key discoveries and key dates give authority to an essay.

Finished Sample Essay

A major change that has occurred in the Western family is an increased incidence in divorce. Whereas in the past, divorce was a relatively rare occurrence, in recent times it has become quite commonplace. For example, in the United States in 1920, only 1.6 per 1,000 people divorced. In 2014, the figure was 3.2 in 1,000 (CDC, NCHS National Vital Statistics System). According to the American Psychological Association, about 40 to 50 percent of marriages end in divorce. A consequence of this change has been a substantial increase in the number of single-parent families and the attendant problems that this brings (Kilmartin, 1997).

An important issue for sociologists, and indeed for all of society, is why these changes in marital patterns have occurred. In this essay I will seek to critically examine a number of sociological explanations for the "divorce phenomenon" and also consider the social policy implications that each explanation carries with it. It will be argued that the best explanations are to be found within a broad socio-economic framework.

One type of explanation for rising divorce has focused on changes in laws relating to marriage. For example, Bilton, Bonnett, and Jones (1987) argue that increased rates of divorce do not necessarily indicate that families are now more unstable. It is possible, they claim, that there has always been a degree of marital instability.

They suggest that changes in the law have been significant, because they have provided unhappily married couples with "access to a legal solution to pre-existent marital problems" (p. 301). Bilton et al. therefore believe that changes in divorce rates can be best explained in terms of changes in the legal system. The problem with this type of explanation, however, is that it does not consider why these laws have changed in the first place. It could be argued that reforms to family law, as well as the increased rate of divorce that has accompanied them, are the product of more fundamental changes in society.

Another type of explanation is one that focuses precisely on these broad societal changes. For example, Nicky Hart (cited in Haralambos, 1995) argues that increases in divorce and marital breakdown are the result of economic changes that have affected the family. One example of these changes is the raised material aspirations of families, which Hart suggests has put pressure on both spouses to become wage earners. Women as a result have been forced to become both homemakers and economic providers. According to Hart, the contradiction of these two roles has led to conflict and this is the main cause of marital breakdown. It would appear that Hart's explanation cannot account for all cases of divorce—for example, marital breakdown is liable to occur in families where only the husband is working. Nevertheless, her approach, which is to relate changes in family relations to broader social forces, would seem to be more probing than one that looks only at legislative change.

The two explanations described above have very different implications for social policy, especially in relation to how the problem of increasing marital instability might be dealt with. Bilton et al. (1995) offer a legal explanation and hence would see the solutions also being determined in this domain. If rises in divorce are thought to be the consequence of liberal divorce laws, the obvious way to stem this rise is to make them less obtainable. This approach, one imagines, would lead to a reduction in divorce statistics; however, it cannot really be held up as a genuine solution to the problems of marital stress and breakdown in society. Indeed it would seem to be a solution directed more at symptoms than addressing fundamental causes. Furthermore, the experience of social workers working in the area of family welfare suggests that restricting a couple's access to divorce would in some cases serve only to exacerbate existing marital problems (Johnson, 1981). In those cases where violence is involved, the consequences could be tragic. Apart from all this, returning to more restrictive divorce laws seems to be a solution little favoured by Australians (Harrison, 1990).

Hart (cited in Haralambos, 1995), writing from a Marxist-feminist position, traces marital conflict to changes in the capitalist economic system and their resultant effect on the roles of men and women. It is difficult to know, however, how such an analysis might be translated into practical social policies. This is because the Hart program would appear to require in the first place a radical restructuring of the economic system. Whilst this may be desirable for some, it is not achievable in the present political climate. Hart is right, however, to suggest that much marital conflict can be linked in some way to the economic circumstances of families. This is borne out in many statistical surveys which show consistently that rates of divorce are higher among socially disadvantaged families (McDonald, 1993). This situation suggests then that social policies need to be geared to providing support and security for these types of families. It is little cause for optimism, however, that in recent years governments of all persuasions have shown an increasing reluctance to fund social welfare programs of this kind.

It is difficult to offer a comprehensive explanation for the grow-ing trend of marital breakdown; and it is even more difficult to find solutions that might ameliorate the problems created by it. Clearly though, as I have argued in this essay, the most useful answers are to be found not within a narrow legal framework, but within a broader socioeconomic one.

Finally, whilst we may appear to be living in a time of increased family instability, research suggests that, historically, instability may have been the norm rather than the exception. As Bell and Zajdow (1997) point out, in the past, single-parent and stepfamilies were more common than is assumed—although the disruptive influence then was not divorce, but the premature death of one or both parents. This situation suggests that in studying the modern family, one needs to employ a historical perspective, including looking to the past in searching for ways of dealing with problems in the present.

References

Australian Bureau of Statistics (1996). *Divorces, Australia*. Canberra: Australian Government Printing Service.

Bell, R., and G. Zajdow (1997). "Family and Household." In R. Jureidini, S. Kenny, and M. Poole (eds.). *Sociology: Australian Connections*. St. Leonards, New South Wales: Allen & Unwin.

Bilton, T., K. Bonnett, and P. Jones (1987). *Introductory Sociology*, 2nd edition. London: Macmillan.

Haralambos, M. (1995). *Sociology: Themes and Perspectives*, 3rd edition. London: Bell & Hyman.

Harrison, M. (1995). "Grounds for Divorce." *Family Matters*. No. 42, pp. 34–35.

Johnson, V. (1981). *The Last Resort: A Women's Refuge*. Ringwood, Australia: Penguin.

Kilmartin, C. (1997). "Children, Divorce and One-Parent Families." *Family Matters*. No. 48, pp. 34–35.

McDonald, P. (1993). *Family Trends and Structure in Australia*. Australian Family Briefings No. 3. Melbourne: Australian Institute of Family Studies.

www.apa.org/topics/divorce

www.cdc.gov/nchs/nvss/marriage_divorce_tables.htm

Sometimes It *Is* Rocket Science

It should be clear by now how mind maps can really help condense many points of information to keep you focused on the sum of its parts. Just for fun I thought of creating a mind map for a chapter on rocket science taken from the NASA website, which you can find here: *www.grc.nasa.gov/WWW/K-12/rocket/rktfor.html.*

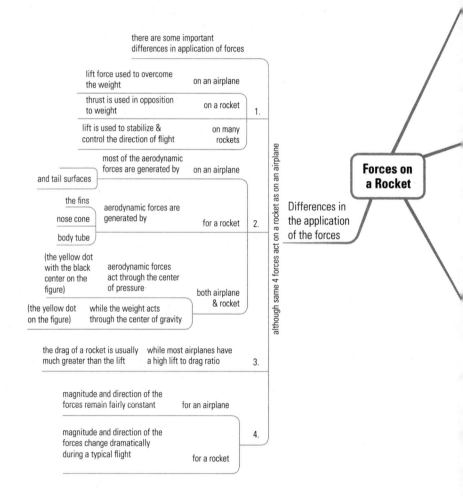

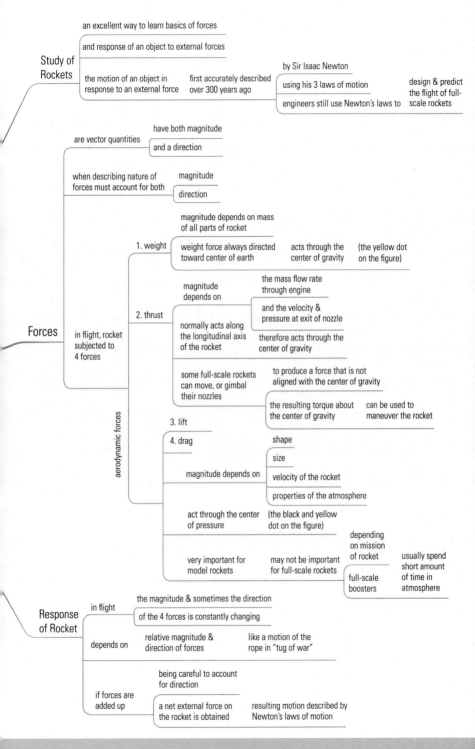

Study of Rockets

- an excellent way to learn basics of forces
- and response of an object to external forces
- the motion of an object in response to an external force
  - first accurately described over 300 years ago
    - by Sir Isaac Newton
    - using his 3 laws of motion
    - engineers still use Newton's laws to design & predict the flight of full-scale rockets

Forces

- are vector quantities
  - have both magnitude
  - and a direction
- when describing nature of forces must account for both
  - magnitude
  - direction
- in flight, rocket subjected to 4 forces
  - 1. weight
    - magnitude depends on mass of all parts of rocket
    - weight force always directed toward center of earth
    - acts through the center of gravity
    - (the yellow dot on the figure)
  - 2. thrust
    - magnitude depends on
      - the mass flow rate through engine
      - and the velocity & pressure at exit of nozzle
    - normally acts along the longitudinal axis of the rocket
      - therefore acts through the center of gravity
    - some full-scale rockets can move, or gimbal their nozzles
      - to produce a force that is not aligned with the center of gravity
      - the resulting torque about the center of gravity
        - can be used to maneuver the rocket

  - aerodynamic forces
    - 3. lift
    - 4. drag
      - magnitude depends on
        - shape
        - size
        - velocity of the rocket
        - properties of the atmosphere
      - act through the center of pressure
        - (the black and yellow dot on the figure)
      - very important for model rockets
        - may not be important for full-scale rockets
          - depending on mission of rocket
          - full-scale boosters
            - usually spend short amount of time in atmosphere

Response of Rocket

- in flight
  - the magnitude & sometimes the direction
  - of the 4 forces is constantly changing
- depends on
  - relative magnitude & direction of forces
    - like a motion of the rope in "tug of war"
- if forces are added up
  - being careful to account for direction
  - a net external force on the rocket is obtained
    - resulting motion described by Newton's laws of motion

KEY POINTS

- Make time to learn things you want to, not just need to, to free your mind from everyday routine.
- Keep at it and get others involved. Social learning makes you learn even faster.
- Use mind mapping to organize writing projects for articles, essays, and reports.
- Don't ever stop learning. It provides fuel for the soul and change in the world.

CHAPTER 8

SPEAKING TO AN AUDIENCE

"Of all of our inventions for mass communication, pictures still speak the most universally understood language."—Walt Disney

MAKING INFORMATION MEMORABLE for others is what communication is all about, and it's the fourth and final step of the Yellow Elephant Memory Model. What is memorable for ourselves, however, may not work for others. Everyone learns differently and information can be perceived in many ways, so it's important to think not only about the information you're providing but also how you'll communicate that to an audience.

Making Speeches Memorable

Many people in the world fear public speaking, and for many different reasons. Memory techniques allow you to be confident that your information is safely stored in your head and accessible, which helps you present with conviction and hopefully settles nerves. Here are some quick tips to help you present that material with confidence.

Know Your Audience

This allows you to really tailor your message. Always ask ahead for as many details as you can, such as the number of people expected, their age demographic, the types of jobs they have, and, if possible, what they hope to get from the presentation.

Know Your Key Message

In one sentence determine what it is that you're trying to say to your audience. If you struggle to do this, then you need to simplify your message.

Plan

Write down all the things you will talk about and create a mind map to quickly identify the main subject areas so you can then develop your content.

Time

Once you have mapped out your talk, work out how long the sections will take. With practice these estimates become fairly accurate.

Prepare

If you have time, practice your presentation in front of a mirror or family and friends, or tape yourself talking. This will help you evaluate your vocal projection and diction, and show if your body language needs some work and if you're rushing things or are too slow.

Deliver

If you've done all your preparation this should be easy. Of course nerves, technical problems, hecklers, roadwork outside, and other disruptions could still occur so your best defense is to know your message really well. Memorize your keywords, themes, and approach. This is better than memorizing your entire talk word for word because you can present it naturally in different ways. People don't want to see a robot talking; they want to see a human speaking. It is far more engaging and builds trust.

Get Feedback

Comments—whether they are great, constructive, or negative—provide opportunities for you to improve in areas that you might not even have been aware of such as mumbling or needing to ask more questions from the audience. No feedback means you only take away what *you* have experienced.

Reflect and Improve

Not many presenters reflect on their speech once it's over. But taking the time to review your speech provides you with ways to improve it so next time it's even better.

The Use of Narrative Illustrations

Think of presentations where the screen is filled with text and the presenter drones on, reading out every single word, neglecting to add any images to break up the words and create some variety. How dull! These types of talks are trapped in the first step of the Yellow Elephant Memory Model: without images the presentation cannot move to the second step.

Just as mind maps can be used to summarize large volumes of information in an organized way, so too can illustrations. These techniques mirror the Yellow Elephant Memory Model because the abstract spoken word is transformed into images, which then tell a story. This is what you often find in comics and graphic novels but they're increasingly being used to help presentations. Check out a few of the sites listed in the Sources section at the back of this book.

How It Works

The following excerpt is from *The Elements of Style* by Strunk and White.

IV. A FEW MATTERS OF FORM

Headings. Leave a blank line, or its equivalent in space, after the title or heading of a manuscript. On succeeding pages, if using ruled paper, begin on the first line.

Numerals. Do not spell out dates or other serial numbers. Write them in figures or in Roman notation, as may be appropriate.

August 9, 1918

Chapter XII

352nd Infantry

Parentheses. A sentence containing an expression in parenthesis is punctuated, outside of the marks of parenthesis, exactly as if the expression in parenthesis were absent. The expression within is punctuated as if it stood by itself, except that the final period is omitted unless it is a question mark or *an exclamation point.*

I went to his house yesterday (my third attempt to see him), but he had left town.

He declares (and why should we doubt his good faith?) that he is now certain of success.

(When a *wholly* detached expression or sentence is parenthesized, the final period comes before the last mark of parenthesis.)

Quotations. Formal quotations, cited as documentary evidence, are introduced by a colon and enclosed in quotation marks.

The provision of the Constitution is: "No tax or duty shall be laid on articles exported from any state."

Quotations grammatically in apposition or the direct objects of verbs are preceded by a comma and enclosed in quotation marks.

I recall the maxim of La Rochefoucauld, "Gratitude is a lively sense of benefits to come."

Aristotle says, "Art is an imitation of nature."

Quotations of an entire line, or more, of verse, are begun on a fresh line and centered, but need not be enclosed in quotation marks.

Wordsworth's enthusiasm for the Revolution was at first unbounded:

Bliss was it in that dawn to be alive,

But to be young was very heaven!

Quotations introduced by *that* are regarded as in indirect discourse and not enclosed in quotation marks.

Keats declares that beauty is truth, truth beauty.

Proverbial expressions and familiar phrases of literary origin require no quotation marks. The same is true of colloquialisms and slang.

These are the times that try men's souls.

References. In scholarly work requiring exact references, abbreviate titles that occur frequently, giving the full forms in an alphabetical list at the end. As a general practice, give the references in parenthesis or in footnotes, not in the body of the sentence. Omit the words *act*, *scene*, *line*, *book*, *volume*, *page*, except when referring by only one of them. Punctuate as indicated below.

| In the second scene of the third act | In III.ii (still better, simply insert III.ii in parenthesis at the proper place in the sentence) |

After the killing of Polonius, Hamlet is placed under guard (IV.ii. 14).

2 Samuel i:17–27

Syllabication. If there is room at the end of a line for one or more syllables of a word, but not for the whole word, divide the word, unless this involves cutting off only a single letter, or cutting off only two letters of a long word. No hard and fast rule for all words can be laid down. The principles most frequently applicable are:

(a) Divide the word according to its formation:

know-ledge (not knowl-edge); Shake-speare (not Shakespeare); de-scribe (not des-cribe); atmo-sphere (not atmos-phere);

(b) Divide "on the vowel":

edi-ble (not ed-ible); propo-sition; ordi-nary; espe-cial; reli-gious; oppo-nents; regu-lar; classi-fi-ca-tion (three divisions allowable); deco-rative; presi-dent;

(c) Divide between double letters, unless they come at the end of the simple form of the word:

Apen-nines; Cincin-nati; refer-ring; but tell-ing.

(d) Do not divide before final –*ed* if the *e* is silent:

treat-ed (but not roam-ed or nam-ed).

The treatment of consonants in combination is best shown from examples:

for-tune; pic-ture; sin-gle; presump-tuous; illus-tration; sub-stan-tial (either division); indus-try; instruc-tion; sug-ges-tion.

The student will do well to examine the syllable-division in a number of pages of any carefully printed book.

Titles. For the titles of literary works, scholarly usage prefers italics with capitalized initials. The usage of editors and publishers varies, some using italics with capitalized initials, others using Roman with capitalized initials and with or without quotation marks. Use italics except in writing for a periodical that follows a different practice. Omit initial *A* or *The* from titles when you place the possessive before them.

The *Iliad*; The *Odyssey; As You Like It; To a Skylark; The Newcomes; A Tale of Two Cities;* Dickens's *Tale of Two Cities.*

Now compare the text against a mind map version of the same content.

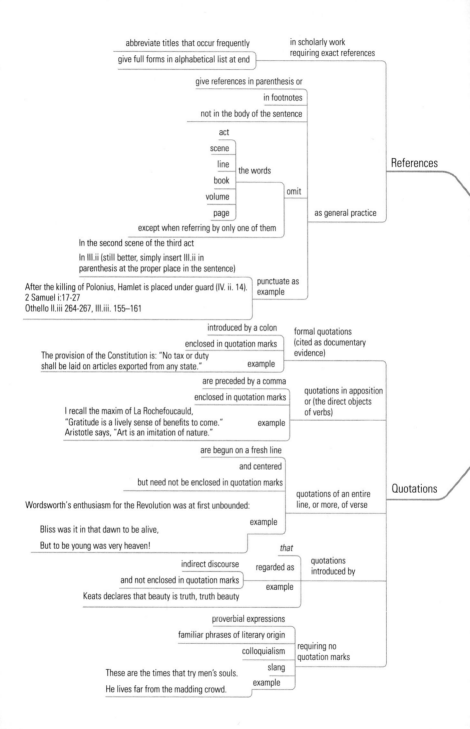

References

- abbreviate titles that occur frequently
- give full forms in alphabetical list at end

— in scholarly work requiring exact references

- give references in parenthesis or
- in footnotes
- not in the body of the sentence

omit the words
- act
- scene
- line
- book
- volume
- page

except when referring by only one of them

— as general practice

punctuate as example:

In the second scene of the third act

In III.ii (still better, simply insert III.ii in parenthesis at the proper place in the sentence)

After the killing of Polonius, Hamlet is placed under guard (IV. ii. 14).
2 Samuel i:17-27
Othello II.iii 264-267, III.iii. 155–161

Quotations

- introduced by a colon
- enclosed in quotation marks

formal quotations (cited as documentary evidence)

example:
The provision of the Constitution is: "No tax or duty shall be laid on articles exported from any state."

- are preceded by a comma
- enclosed in quotation marks

quotations in apposition or (the direct objects of verbs)

example:
I recall the maxim of La Rochefoucauld, "Gratitude is a lively sense of benefits to come."
Aristotle says, "Art is an imitation of nature."

- are begun on a fresh line
- and centered
- but need not be enclosed in quotation marks

quotations of an entire line, or more, of verse

example:
Wordsworth's enthusiasm for the Revolution was at first unbounded:

Bliss was it in that dawn to be alive,

But to be young was very heaven!

quotations introduced by *that*

- regarded as indirect discourse
- and not enclosed in quotation marks

example:
Keats declares that beauty is truth, truth beauty

- proverbial expressions
- familiar phrases of literary origin
- colloquialism
- slang

requiring no quotation marks

example:
These are the times that try men's souls.
He lives far from the madding crowd.

IV. A Few Matters of Form

Headings
- after title or heading of a manuscript
  - leave a blank line
  - or equivalent in space
- on succeeding pages
  - if using ruled paper, begin on the first line

Numerals
- do not
  - spell out dates
  - or other serial numbers
- write in
  - figures
  - roman notation
  - example
    - August 9, 1918 (9 August 1918)
    - Rule 3
    - Chapter XII
    - 352nd Infantry

Parentheses
- a sentence containing an expression in parenthesis
  - is punctuated
    - outside of the marks of parenthesis
    - exactly as if expression in parenthesis were absent
- the expression within
  - is punctuated as if it stood by itself
  - except that the final stop is omitted
    - unless it is a question mark
    - or an exclamation point
- example
  - I went to his house yesterday (my third attempt to see him), but he had left town
  - He declares (and why should we doubt his good faith?) that he is now certain of success

KEY POINTS

- Know your key message when presenting.
- Rehearse your presentation.
- Use imagery, stories, and keywords as triggers for your talk.
- Double-check content before you speak or press send. Will the audience or reader easily understand it?
- Use mind maps or illustrations to help encode big blocks of data.

CHAPTER 9

LEARNING LANGUAGES

"Learning never exhausts the mind."—Leonardo da Vinci

LEARNING ANOTHER LANGUAGE opens a door to a new culture and expands your assumptions of how other people, often very different from you, live their lives. It also demonstrates to everyone your dedication and discipline, which may result in other, extra benefits and opportunities. There are, however, a lot of reasons people use to explain why they've not managed to learn another language, many of them similar to those made in Chapter 5.

Roadblocks to Success: Negative Self-Talk
"It's Too Difficult"
I used to believe Chinese was an extremely difficult language to learn because of its bewildering written text with its vast number of characters, and its unfamiliar sounds when spoken. But when I began studying it, I found some principles were

easier to understand than with English. You never know unless you give it a try.

"I Don't Have the Time"

People are busy and time is precious. Most people, though, don't know how to use their free time effectively. New technologies are also needlessly keeping us busier as well as wasting our time.

And what if learning a language wasn't so difficult or time-consuming?

In 2013 I spent a year as a participant in the Asialink Leaders Program. This program allows leaders in a range of professional fields to initiate projects that engage and build stronger Asia–Australia relationships. As the "memory expert" I wanted to apply memory techniques to learn Chinese Mandarin in the most effective and efficient way possible.

I couldn't begin by opening any book on Mandarin and memorizing but instead had to develop a plan, similar to the one I used to memorize the *Yellow Pages*. I knew I had to:

- Develop a memory strategy
- Choose the most suitable memory techniques
- Develop a learning program incorporating the techniques
- Test it myself

This project helped me develop a template not just for learning Mandarin, but for *any* language. And the cool part is that if you spend forty minutes a day on this you'll be speaking the language within a month.

How It Works

Many people believe we need to learn and memorize vocabulary to learn and speak a language. While this may be true in one sense, memorizing hundreds or even thousands of words doesn't mean that you'll learn the language. This is because words on their own have no context and meanings can differ enormously depending on the situation. When we were children, our parents spoke to us with phrases like "Come here," "Hello, how are you?" and "What on earth are you doing?" (Okay, the last one was inspired by my wife dealing with my four-year-old.)

We learned our mother tongue through repeated phrases, so it makes sense for us to memorize *phrases* instead of individual *words*. The difference between remembering through rote learning (the repetition of phrases) and memory techniques is time. You may repeat phrases hundreds of times, while memory techniques may only require three or four repetitions. Memory techniques enable you to learn much faster, with better long-term recognition. Memorizing phrases helps us learn things in context and gets us speaking much faster than if learning individual words. The concept is: the more phrases you memorize, the more language you will be able to speak.

To begin, you will need to do three things:

1. Learn and memorize the pronunciations
2. Memorize the phrases
3. Review phrases

If you don't learn the correct pronunciation then the memory connections you make will be incorrect. Yes, you'll likely remember them, but you'll end up saying the wrong thing! It is *essential* to spend time memorizing the pronunciations, and this is especially the case for languages that are tonal like Chinese. Tonal languages use different pitches to distinguish meaning. Memorize the wrong pitch, and you could be offending someone instead of asking her name.

Chinese Mandarin
Pinyin System
This system was designed to translate the pronunciation of Chinese characters phonetically. Pinyin is Chinese for "spelled-out sounds."

Pronunciations

b	Similar to "b" in "boat," softened to a "p" sound.
p	Similar to "p" in "top"—with more finality.
m	Same as "m" in the English "ma."
f	Same as "f" in the English "fat."
d	Similar to "d" in the English "down": softened to approach a "t" sound.
t	Similar to "t" in the English "top."
n	Similar to "n" in the English "name."
l	Similar to "l" in the English "look."
g	Similar to "g" in the English "go": softened to approach a "k" sound.
k	Similar to "k" in the English "kiss."
h	Similar to "h" in the English "hope."
j	Similar to "j" in the English "jeep": tongue is positioned below lower teeth.
q	Similar to "ch" in the English "cheap": tongue is positioned below lower teeth.
x	Similar to "sh" in the English "sheep": tongue is positioned below lower teeth.

zh	Similar to "j" in the English "jam."
ch	Similar to "ch" in the English "cheap."
sh	Similar to "sh" in the English "ship."
r	Similar to "z" in the English "azure."
z	Same as "ds" in the English "woods."
c	Similar to "ts" in the English "bits."
s	Similar to "s" in the English "see."
(y)i	Similar to "ee" in the English "bee."
(w)u	Similar to "oo" in the English "room."
yu	Purse your lips and position the tongue high and forward.
a	Similar to "ah" in the English "Ah-ha!"
(w)o	Similar to "or" in the English "bore."
e	Similar to "er" in the English "hers."
(y)e	Similar to the English "Yay!"
ai	Similar to the English "eye."
ei	Similar to "ei" in the English "weigh."
ao	Similar to "au" in "sauerkraut."
ou	Similar to "ou" in "dough."
an	Similar to "an" in "fan."
en	Similar to "un" in "under."
ang	A Mandarin "a" followed by the "ng" sound like in the English "sing."
eng	A Mandarin "e" followed by the "ng" sound like in the English "sing."
er	A Mandarin "e" with the tongue curled back.

Tonal System

There are five tones in Chinese Mandarin, which are critical to understand as you learn to speak the language. Warning: if the tone you use is incorrect you'll be saying something *completely* different from what you meant to say.

1. Level monotone   mā   (mother)

The tone is consistent, just like opening your mouth at the dentist and saying "ahhhhh."

2. Rising tone   má   (hemp)

The tone rises up as if asking a question: what?

3. Dips down then up   mǎ   (horse)

The tone dips down and then back up again, like stretching out the word "door": doo—oor.

4. Fast fall down   mà   (scold)

The tone quickly dips down, similar to saying "the" quickly.

5. Neutral: no emphasis   ma

Sounds as it is read, like "meh"—like you just don't care.

How to Memorize Chinese Phrases

Use the Yellow Elephant association techniques to help you.

Abstract: Nǐ hǎo ma: How are you?

Image: Nǐ (knee) hǎo (how) ma (ma: as in mother)

Association: You hit your "knee" on the table and started to scream in pain.
You hear a voice behind you asking: "Howww" did you do that?" You turn
around and see that it was your "ma," who then says, "How are you?"

French

Many of us likely began to study French at school but gave up after a couple of years. This romance language shares many similarities with English, and the same alphabet certainly helps.

Pronunciation

Vowels

a, à, â	Similar to "a" in "card."
e	Similar to "a" in "around."
é	Similar to "ay" in "lay."
ê, è	Similar to "e" in "get."
i, î	Similar to "ee" in "deed."
o, o, ô, au, eau	Similar to "oh" or "aw" in "saw."
ou	Similar to "oo" in "food."
u, ù	Similar to "ew" in "few."
y	Similar to "ee" in "deed."

Consonants

b	Same as "b" in "bed."
c	Same as "c" in "color."
ç	Similar to "s" in "sit."
d	Same as "d" in "dog."
f	Same as "f" in "fit."
g	Same as "g" in "get."
h	This is a silent letter.
j	Similar to "g" in "orange."
k	Same as "k" in "kite."
l	Same as "l" in "luck."
m	Same as "m" in "mine."
n	Same as "n" in "nose."
p	Same as "p" in "peach."
q(u)	Same as "k" in "kite."
r	Similar to first "r" in "rare."
s	Same as "s" in "sat."
t	Same as "t" in "take."

v	Same as "v" in "viper."
x	Same as "x" in "exit."
z	Same as "z" in "zip."

Gliding Vowels (Diphthongs)

ail	Similar to "i" in "light."
ais	Similar to "ea" in "head."
au, eau	Similar to "oh."
an	Similar to "ahng," without the "g."
eu	Similar to "oo" in "poodle."
œ	Similar to "e" in "me," but faster.
er	Sounds like "air."
ez	Similar to "ay" in "lay."
en, em	Nasal sound; same as "an."
in	Nasal sound; like "ang" in "gang," without the "g."
oi	Similar to "wa" in "wander."
oin	Nasal sound; like "ang" in "gang," without the "g."
ou	Similar to "oo" in "fool."
on	Nasal sound; like "ong" in "thong," without the "g."
oui	Similar to "wee" in "weep."
ui	Similar to "wee" in "weep," but with the tongue forward.
un	Nasal sound; like "ung" in "lung," without the "l."
ch	Similar to "sh" in "push."
gn	Similar to "ny" in "canyon."
il	Similar to "y" in "years."
ll	Similar to "l."
ph	Similar to "f" in "fan."
tch	Similar to the "ch" in "chess."
th	Similar to the "t" in "tap."
tr	The "t" followed by rolling of the tongue.

How to Memorize French Phrases

Abstract: Comment allez-vous? How are you?

Image: Comment (comment) allez (Ali) vouz (you)

Association: A really funny "comment" was made to "Ali." He turned around and asked "How are you?" to the person making the remarks.

It will take some time at first to come up with associations for the foreign words, but a minute or two is all that's needed to make up a story connecting the phrase similar to the previous example. The more you practice, the better you will get.

Try to visualize the story and the sounds around you and you won't need to repeat phrases a hundred times to learn them. A simple association with some emotion will make things so much faster and you'll be well on your way to learning any language in record time.

Learning 1,500 phrases will have you speaking the language at its very basic form. If you spend around forty minutes a day memorizing twenty-five phrases then you'll pick up the spoken language in two months. That is less than forty-eight hours' study! If you like, you can build on this with seventeen phrases a day for three months. This system means that you can learn to speak any language within months, not years.

Test Your Skills

Try your memorization skills with the following Mandarin and French phrases.

Pinyin	English
Juéduì bú shì.	Absolutely not.
Nǐ gēn wǒ yìqǐ qù ma?	Are you coming with me?
Nǐ néng kěndìng ma?	Are you sure?
Kuài dàole ma?	Are we almost there?
Jìnkuài.	As soon as possible.
Xiāngxìn wǒ.	Believe me.
Mǎi xià lái!	Buy it!
Míngtiān dǎ diànhuà gěi wǒ.	Call me tomorrow.
Qǐng nín shuō de màn xiē hǎo ma?	Can you speak slowly?
Gēn wǒ lái.	Come with me.
Gōngxǐ gōngxǐ.	Congratulations.
Bǎ tā zuò duì.	Do it right!
Nǐ dàngzhēn?	Do you mean it?
Nǐ jīngcháng jiàn dào tā ma?	Do you see him often?
Nǐ míngbái le ma?	Do you understand?
Nǐ yào ma?	Do you want it?
Nǐ xiǎng yào xiē shénme?	Do you want something?
Bú yào zuò.	Don't do it.
Bú yào kuāzhāng.	Don't exaggerate.
Bú yào gàosu wǒ.	Don't tell me that.
Bāng wǒ yíxià.	Give me a hand.
Yīzhí wǎng qián.	Go right ahead.
Zhù lǚtú yúkuài.	Have a good trip.
Zhù nǐ yì tiān guò de yúkuài.	Have a nice day.
Zài lái yígè.	Have another one.
Nǐ zuò wán le ma?	Have you finished?
Tā méi kòng.	He doesn't have time.
Tā xiànzài yǐjīng zài lù shàng le.	He is on his way.

Nǐ hǎo ma?	How are you doing?
Nǐ yào dāi duōjiǔ?	How long are you staying?
Duōshǎo qián?	How much?
Wǒ duì tā zháomí le.	I am crazy about her.
Wǒ zài làngfèi shíjiān.	I am wasting my time.
Wǒ néng zuò.	I can do it.
Wǒ jiǎnzhí bùnéng xiāngxìn.	I can't believe it.
Wǒ bù néng zài děng le.	I can't wait.
Wǒ méi shíjiān le.	I don't have time.
Wǒ yī gè rén dōu bú rènshi.	I don't know anybody.
Wǒ bù xǐhuan.	I don't like it.
Wǒ rènwéi búshì.	I don't think so.

French	English
Merci beaucoup.	Thank you very much.
Vous parlez français?	Do you speak French? *(formal)*
Pourriez-vous parler plus lentement, s'il vous plaît?	Could you speak more slowly, please?
Pourriez-vous me l'écrire, s'il vous plaît?	Could you write it down for me, please?
Je ne comprends pas.	I don't understand.
Je ne sais pas.	I don't know.
À demain!	See you tomorrow!
Excusez-moi, où sont les toilettes?	Excuse me, where's the toilet?
Bonne journée!	Have a nice day!
J'ai un petit nez et un visage rond.	I have a small nose and a round face.
Tu as le visage très rouge.	Your face is very red.
J'aime le chocolat mais je n'aime pas le lait.	I like chocolate but I don't like milk.

Qu'est-ce que vous voulez boire?	What would you like to drink?
Je cherche le centre commercial.	I am looking for the shopping mall.
Combien coûte le billet?	How much is a ticket?
Je peux essayer cette robe?	May I try on this dress?
Pouvez-vous m'aider?	Can you help me?
Très bien. Je vous souhaite une bonne journée, Mademoiselle.	All right. Have a good day, Miss.
De quoi souffrez-vous?	What's wrong with you?
Vous prenez la carte de crédit?	Do you take credit cards?

KEY POINTS

- Make sure you memorize the pronunciations before memorizing phrases. It will make learning much more effective.
- Take your time and don't rush making associations for phrases. Use the SMASHIN' SCOPE technique to help you.
- Visualize the end goal of speaking the language. How will it feel to communicate with someone in their language? Use this as motivation to keep you going.
- Have fun making silly stories for characters and phrases.
- Make sure you can practice with someone who speaks the language. You don't want to be memorizing for hours only to have done it incorrectly!
- Don't worry about getting the exact memory associations for words or phrases. Even making an association to the first letter can be enough to trigger the rest of the word.

CHAPTER 10

LEARNING MUSIC

"One good thing about music—when it hits you,
you feel no pain."—Bob Marley

LEARNING TO PLAY a musical instrument is often at the top of people's wish list of things to do, but most just don't get around to it. I taught myself how to play guitar, and back in the day played in a band in front of thousands as well as recorded in studios. And there are many famous self-taught guitarists such as Keith Richards, Jimi Hendrix, Prince, and Eddie Van Halen. I'm not saying ditch the lessons, because learning the fundamentals and music theory will give you musical know-how and many more ideas on how to make your own music. But if you just want to play then it makes good sense to start with a simple approach.

The Guitar

Most people will have some idea of how to hold a guitar. Usually it rests on your leg (right, if you're right-handed) and is kept close to your body, upright and straight. It's important not to slouch as it will make you tire more easily.

You can play individual notes and chords on a guitar, though here we'll focus on individual notes so you become familiar with the instrument.

How It Works: Using Tablature

An easy way to play notes, even if you don't know them, is to use guitar tablature. Tablature shows you where to place your fingers on the guitar. Here is part of *Für Elise* by Beethoven:

Part 1 (Play this whole section twice)

```
E--12-11-12-11-12-7-10-8-5-------5-7---------7-8---0--
B---------------------------5----------9----------
G------------------------5-----------9-----------
D--------------------------------------------------
A--------------------------------------------------
E--------------------------------------------------
```

The letters represent the notes and string types. The first string starts from the bottom E, then second string is A, then D, G, B, and the sixth string, E. You don't need to memorize these—you just need to know that the first string is the thickest string, and the thinnest string is the sixth string.

This means that *Für Elise* starts with placing your finger on and playing the twelfth fret on the sixth string, then the eleventh fret on the sixth string, and back to the twelfth fret. A 0 on a line means playing an open string. Try playing the rest of *Für Elise*. Once you master the guitar tablature, you can memorize the tablature using the Major or Dominic systems.

```
E----12-11-12-11-12-7-10-8-5-------5-7---0-8-7-5------
B----------------------------5------------------
G---------------------------5-------------------
D-----------------------------------------------
A-----------------------------------------------
E-----------------------------------------------
```

Part 2

```
E-7-8-10-12----13-12-10----12-10-8--0-10-8-7--0-0-12-0-12-12--11-
B--------------------------------------------------------------
G-----------12----------10-------------------------------------
D--------------------------------------------------------------
A--------------------------------------------------------------
E--------------------------------------------------------------
```

Part 1b

```
E--12-11-12-11-12-11-12-11-12-11-12-7-10-8-5-------5-7---------7-8---0--
B-------------------------------------------5----------9---------
G-------------------------------------5----------9-----------
D------------------------------------------------------------
A------------------------------------------------------------
E------------------------------------------------------------
```

How It Works: Using the Major System

Let's look at ways to use the number systems to memorize guitar scales, chord progressions, and aspects of music theory. You can memorize the start of *Für Elise* with the Major System:

12-11-12-11-12-7-10-8-5

Tin-Toad-Tin-Toad-Tin-Key-Toes-Woof-Lie

5 = l, 7 = k, 8 = f, 10 = ts, 11 = td, 12 = tn

Picture giving a **tin** can of food to a **toad**. He doesn't like it and throws the **tin** back. You walk up to the **toad** and ask why he didn't like the **tin**? He tells you that he needs a **key** to open it. You wiggle your **toes** and magically the can opens. Much to both your surprise, there is a loud **woof** sound coming from inside. You both **lie** on the floor in shock.

This memory technique also works very well to remember guitar scales as follows:

C Ionian starting from the A-string

```
e:-----------------------------------5-7-8----------------------|
B:------------------------------5-6-8---------------------------|
G:-----------------------4-5-7----------------------------------|
D:----------------3-5-7----------------------------------------|
A:---------3-5-7-----------------------------------------------|
E:-----------------------------------------------------------|
```

If we create words in groups of three digits using the Major System, we get the following:

```
357(milk), 357(milk), 457(relic), 568(leech-off), 578(liquefy)
       3 = m, 4 = r, 5 = l, 6 = ch, 7 = k and q, 8 = f
```

Picture **Dora** the Explorer drinking her **milk**. She loves it so much she's going for a second helping of **milk**. As she reaches into the fridge for the carton, she takes out an old **relic** instead. From inside the relic out jumps a huge leech that latches on to Dora. She tells the **leech off** for scaring her and **liquefies** it with help from her trusty monkey Boots.

The Keyboard

Piano lessons have been a part of many people's lives for generations. Today the piano is still one of the most popular instruments to play. According to a 2010 *LA Times* article, six-year-olds who received keyboard instruction had more brain growth and finer motor skills than their peers. The piece also stated that "learning to make music changes the brain and boosts broad academic performance." So to sharpen the mind and improve memory, learn to play music rather than just listen to it.

For those of you otherwise unfamiliar with the keyboard, let's play the song "You Are My Sunshine" by Charles Mitchell and Jimmie Davis.

1. First you need to memorize the notes for the song. The notes are:

C (this one's middle C)

F

G

A

B-flat

C (high C)

D

A simple way of remembering these notes is to group them and make words from them, as in the following.

1	3	4	5	5	5	4	5	3	3
C	F	G	A	A	A	G	A	F	F
5	3	2	1	1	1	2	1	3	3
You	are	my	sun-	shine	my	on-	ly	sun-	shine

1	2	3	4	5	5	4	3	2
F	G	A	B-flat	D	D	C	B-flat	A
5	4	3	2	1	1	2	3	4
you	make	me	hap-	py	when	skies	are	gray

1	2	3	4	5	5	4	3	2	1
F	G	A	B-flat	D	D	C	B-flat	A	F
5	4	3	2	1	1	2	3	4	5
you'll	ne-	ver	know	dear	how	much	I	love	you

1	2	3	4	2	2	3	1
F	G	A	B-flat	G	G	A	F
5	4	3	2	4	4	3	5
please	don't	take	my	sun-	shine	a-	way

I've bunched the letters into groups of three notes, except when it made sense to use four letters to form "GAFF" and complete the phrase for the song. Of course, you can create your own grouping and ordering as long as you can make words out of the letters.

1. CFG   café good
2. AAA   AAA batteries
3. GAFF   making a gaffe (mistake)
4. FGA   fog around
5. BDD   bad day
6. CBA   Commonwealth Bank (Australia)
7. FGA   fog around
8. BDD   bad day
9. CBA   Commonwealth Bank (Australia)
10. FFG   fire and fog
11. ABG   Abigail
12. GAF   gave

To memorize we will need to make a story with the previous words in a sequence:

> It's a beautiful day and the sun is shining. Your local **café** is **good** but you find **AAA batteries** inside your cup. Oops, it looks like someone made a **gaffe** and you've already swallowed them! You try to find the waiter but there is too much **fog around**. Suddenly it's turning into a **bad day** and you race into the nearest **Commonwealth Bank**, but it turns out there is **fog around** inside there as well. This **bad day** looks to continue at the **Commonwealth Bank** because now there is **fire and fog** inside! You stagger outside coughing and a gorgeous lady named **Abigail** approaches. She also happens to be the waiter from the café and tells you whoever **gave** you the coffee will be sacked.

2. The next step is to play the notes memorized in step 1 on the piano. The letters on the keys indicate the notes for the song.

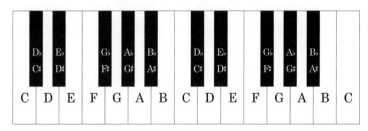

Having memorized the notes allows you to focus on building muscle memory for your fingers so that they start to learn where the notes on the piano are as you play the song.

KEY POINTS

- Work on memorizing notes for songs and then build your muscle memory by applying what you've remembered to play the song.
- Use your finger or, even better, a plectrum to play random notes on the guitar. It doesn't have to make beautiful music; it's just to get your fingers used to the fretboard.
- Websites such as YouTube, Virtual Piano, and GuitarMasterClass offer some great videos on playing piano and guitar that are worth checking out.
- Get some guitar tablatures. You can find plenty online as well as in guitar magazines.
- If you want to, try memorizing the tablature for a song to increase your memory power and exercise your mind.

CHAPTER 11

KNOWING MORE ABOUT . . . EVERYTHING

"Without knowledge action is useless, and knowledge without action is futile."—Abū Bakr al-Ṣiddīq

TODAY WE ARE bombarded by information, meaning we have more to read, more to analyze, more to think about and more to discuss. To stop us feeling overwhelmed by this aspect of modern living we need to organize our information better so we can access it faster and more precisely. With traditional methods of rote learning, acquiring knowledge takes time. In using a systemized approach we can reduce that time and increase our retention of facts and data. Questions to ask include:

- What knowledge are we trying to acquire?
- How many pieces of information are we trying to remember?
- Which technique is the best for the job?

How to Memorize Countries and Their Capitals

The quickest and most effective way to do this is to use a straight linking and association method.

Country	Capital	Association
Morocco	Rabat	You eat a lovely rabbit stew in Morocco.
Gabon	Libreville	You are in a city library where you are asked to keep quiet and not gab on your phone.
Comoros	Moroni	You comb a rose and it transforms into a maroon color.
Latvia	Riga	You work out your lat muscles rigorously in Latvia.
Ecuador	Quito	You will never quit until you reach the equator.
Oman	Muscat	You said "Oh, man!" after tasting the delicious muscat wine.
Switzerland	Bern	Roger Federer burns up the tennis court.
Malaysia	Kuala Lumpur	Koalas come from Malaysia.
Vietnam	Hanoi	You are annoyed when your bike gets stolen in Vietnam.

Some countries are easy to remember while others are more difficult because of the abstract wording of the country or city. Use SMASHIN' SCOPE to help make memorable stories. I may decide, for example, it's stronger for recall if I memorize Libreville, Gabon, by imagining my friend Gabriel standing on a library shelf.

How to Learn Quiz Questions and Answers

To remember quiz questions and their answers:

- Break up keywords into images
- Link each image
- Review the associative story

Example:
> Q. What term describes an adult male swan?
> A. Cob.

The words to associate and connect are: male swan and cob.
> The male swan always eats corn on the cob.

Let's try another.
> Q. What is the largest bone in the human body?
> A. Femur.

The words to associate and connect are: largest bone, human body, femur.

> Picture holding a bone as large as a human. It's so large and heavy that you lose control and drop it on a female.

Try memorizing the following quiz questions and answers:

1. In computing what is RAM short for?
2. Which organ secretes insulin?
3. Who was the first actor to refuse an Oscar?
4. What is the famous business list that *Fortune* produces each year called?
5. What year did Adolf Hitler become chancellor of Germany?
6. Who composed *Peer Gynt*?
7. Who was the youngest ever American president?

8. How many episodes of *Friends* were made?
9. What name is given to the hybrid fruit of tangerines and grapefruits?
10. What do the dots on a pair of dice total?
11. How high is a basketball hoop?
12. In photography what does SLR mean?
13. What is the motto of the U.S. Marines?
14. In what year was prohibition repealed?
15. How many years did Nelson Mandela spend in prison?
16. Which star is the nearest to Earth?
17. What is the nearest galaxy to the solar system?
18. Which nerve forms the link between the eye and the brain?
19. How many species of reptiles live in Antarctica?
20. In which year was the first Super Bowl held?
21. What is agoraphobia the fear of?
22. How many kilograms make up a metric ton?
23. On what date is Independence Day?
24. Who said, "I think, therefore I am?"
25. In which country was inventor Elon Musk born?
26. What was the name of the detective in Agatha Christie's *Murder on the Orient Express*?
27. The clavicle is more commonly known as which bone?
28. What is the collective noun for a group of rhinoceroses?
29. Facing the bow of a boat, which side is port?
30. Who painted *The Starry Night*?

Answers: 1. random-access memory; 2. pancreas; 3. George C. Scott; 4. *Fortune* 500; 5. 1933; 6. Edvard Grieg; 7. Theodore Roosevelt, age forty-two; 8. 236; 9. tangelo; 10. forty-two; 11. ten feet (3.048 m); 12. single lens reflex; 13. Semper Fidelis; 14. 1933; 15. twenty-seven; 16. the Sun; 17. Andromeda; 18. optic nerve; 19. none; 20. 1967; 21. open spaces; 22. 1,000; 23. July 4; 24. René Descartes; 25. South Africa; 26. Hercule Poirot; 27. collarbone; 28. a crash; 29. left; 30. Vincent van Gogh.

How to Memorize Quotes

Good quotes help us reflect on things and can pack a great deal of wisdom into a phrase or brief sentence. They are also one of the most popular forms of shared content on the Internet. As with quiz questions, memorizing quotes uses association, but with the added difficulty of creating images for the person's name.

The approach is to:

- Break up keywords into images
- Link each image
- Connect images to the person

Example:

"You have to dream before your dreams can come true." A.P.J. Abdul Kalam

> Picture someone holding a gun next to your head telling you, **"You have to dream"** or else. So you do that but **before your dream can come true**, you wake up. A man is standing next to you in **A.P.J.** singing Paula **Abdul**. You say: "What a calamity!"

Try memorizing these quotes:

1. *"Start by doing what's necessary; then do what's possible; and suddenly you are doing the impossible."* Saint Francis of Assisi
2. *"The best and most beautiful things in the world cannot be seen or even touched: they must be felt with the heart."* Helen Keller
3. *"It does not matter how slowly you go as long as you do not stop."* Confucius

4. *"Perfection is not attainable, but if we chase perfection we can catch excellence."* Vince Lombardi

5. *"You must be the change you wish to see in the world."* Mahatma Gandhi

6. *"I can't change the direction of the wind, but I can adjust my sails to always reach my destination."* James Dean

7. *"Quality is not an act, it is a habit."* Aristotle

8. *"To the mind that is still, the whole universe surrenders."* Lao Tzu

9. *"Give light, and the darkness will disappear of itself."* Desiderius Erasmus

10. *"If opportunity doesn't knock, build a door."* Milton Berle

How to Memorize Scores and Statistics

Sports fans love a good stat. When considering statistics, identify what you want to remember—there are many facets, such as score, scorers, teams, date, time, and venue.

Soccer

Saturday, March 14, 2015		
Crystal Palace	**3:1**	**Queens Park Rangers**
Wilfried Zaha (CP)	21'	
James McArthur (CP)	40'	
Joel Ward (CP)	42'	
Matt Phillips (QPR)	83'	

In this data, there are eleven different types of information to remember: day, date, month, year, team 1, team 2, team 1 score, team 2 score, goal scorer(s), goal scorer team, and goal in minute of match.

Images will need to be created for each:

Saturday (Saturn)

03 (sumo)

14 (door)

2015 (nose, doll)

Crystal Palace (a large palace made of crystal)

Queens Park Rangers (the queen deploying park rangers)

3:1 (mat)

Wilfried Zaha (Prince William freed a zebra)

21 (net)

James McArthur (Captain James Cook having McDonald's with your friend Arthur)

40 (rose)

Joel Ward (hole in the wall)

42 (Arnie)

Matt Phillips (welcome mat with built-in Phillips head screwdriver)

83 (foam)

Now for the fun in connecting the associative story:

The planet **Saturn** crashes down and falls on top of a **sumo** wrestler at your front **door**, who ends up breaking his **nose**. As he turns around he is greeted by a lovely **doll** inside **a large palace made of crystal**. The **queen** comes out of the palace with her **park rangers** on a long red **mat**. Leading the group is **Prince William** proudly riding his **freed zebra**. From his pocket he casts a **net** at **Captain James Cook**, who is eating **McDonald's** with his mate **Arthur**. Both are trapped. A **rose** starts to appear from a **hole in the wall**—it's **Arnie**. He busts through the wall, jumps on the **welcome mat**, snatching up the **Phillips head screwdriver**, and rescues the two, landing safely on **foam**.

It may seem like a lot of work, but it only takes one story to be developed and visualized for all the details to be stored in your long-term memory. Try creating stories for these statistics:

Friday, June 5, 2015 MLB Scores

Chicago Cubs	5	Washington Nationals	7
Los Angeles Angels	7	New York Yankees	8
San Francisco Giants	5	Philadelphia Phillies	4

Saturday, June 6, 2015 MLB Scores

Houston Astros	2	Toronto Blue Jays	7
Milwaukee Brewers	4	Minnesota Twins	2
Texas Rangers	4	Kansas City Royals	2
Oakland Athletics	2	Boston Red Sox	4
Baltimore Orioles	1	Cleveland Indians	2

Team Statistics: Baseball Scores

To memorize scores, you can include: team 1, team 2, team 1 score, team 2 score, date, and venue.

July 4, 2015 at Fenway Park

Boston Red Sox	6	Houston Astros	1

The associative story would go something like this:

The baseball player was wearing his bright red socks (Red Sox) all the way up toward the stars. Uh oh, Houston, we have a problem! (Astros). Out of the bright red socks came a whole bunch of sticks (6). The baseball player took one stick (1) and threw it into space. The stick went so fast that it traveled back in time and whacked Julius Caesar (July), who collapsed flat on a door (4). This was not a fun way (Fenway) to be entertained, so he went to the park (Park) and played ball.

Individual Player Statistics: 2015 MLB Spring Training

Player Name (Team)	Games Played	At Bats	Runs	Hits	Batting Average
José Abreu (CWS)	19	59	10	30	.508
Curtis Granderson (NYM)	22	52	10	23	.442
Mike Trout (LAA)	**22**	**59**	**22**	**26**	**.441**
Mookie Betts (BOS)	19	56	15	24	.429
John Mayberry Jr. (NYM)	24	53	11	22	.415

Memorize the player's name then link the stats together using any number technique. Using the Major System, our story is:

Mike is on a bike Trout fishing in L.A. and catches an Angel (LAA). It just so happens a nun (22) passing by sees this happen and starts playing an unusual game (Games Played). This game was being played with bats (At Bats) that had lip (59) kiss marks on them. The nun (22) started to run (Runs) but tripped over herself and hit (Hits) the notch (26) of her belt. This batting game was very average (Batting Average) and had indeed reared (441) its ugly head.

Create stories for the following individual player statistics.

2015 MLB Player Statistics (Spring Training)

Player Name (Team)	Games Played	At Bats	Runs	Hits	Batting Average
José Abreu (CWS)	19	59	10	30	.508
Curtis Granderson (NYM)	22	52	10	23	.442
Mike Trout (LAA)	22	59	22	26	.441

Player Name (Team)	Games Played	At Bats	Runs	Hits	Batting Average
Mookie Betts (BOS)	19	56	15	24	.429
John Mayberry Jr. (NYM)	24	53	11	22	.415
C.J. Cron (LAA)	26	75	11	31	.413
Pete Kozma (STL)	24	49	9	20	.408
Lorenzo Cain (KC)	19	55	8	21	.382
Luis Valbuena (HOU)	17	50	4	19	.380
Billy Burns (OAK)	28	83	21	31	.373
A.J. Pollock (ARI)	22	70	12	26	.371
Matt Kemp (SD)	18	54	9	20	.370
David Freese (LAA)	20	55	10	20	.364
Jake Lamb (ARI)	25	66	12	24	.364
Brennan Boesch (CIN)	23	61	9	22	.361
Matt Duffy (SF)	26	61	8	22	.361

KEY POINTS

- Identify what information you want to remember.
- Break down the information into bits to be memorized and create the images for them.
- Consider which technique works best for the task. Linking and association may work just as well as the Method of Loci.
- Practice with large sets of data so you create elaborate stories and connections, and remember more.
- Show off your skills to friends. This is a good way of testing your competence.

CHAPTER 12

BECOME A MEMORY ATHLETE

"The healthiest competition occurs when average people win by putting in above-average effort."—Colin Powell

EACH YEAR PEOPLE of many nations come together for the World Memory Championships, where participants sit and memorize for an allotted time. Once memorization time finishes, a recall period is given allowing competitors to show what they remembered. The purpose of the competition is to see who has the best and most effective memory. It sounds extremely nerdy and only for *really smart* people. That's what I first thought, too, before entering it myself.

When I did, I was shocked to see everyday, average people like you and me doing truly extraordinary things with their brain. This is what the World Memory Championships and this book are all about—the ordinary person doing extraordinary things. What's even more exciting is that the participants don't just remember hundreds of digits or randomly shuffled decks of playing cards; they take away skills to assist them in their everyday life—skills such as fast memorization, brain training for mental performance, and improved concentration and focus. Entering a memory championship will help you with:

- Greater memory and recall
- Improving focus and concentration
- Self-discipline
- Accountability
- Accomplishing goals
- Managing time better
- Completing tasks faster

The World Memory Championships
The World Memory Championships comprise ten distinct events held over three days. Entrants compete in all ten events for the chance to be crowned the World Memory Champion.

1. Names and faces. Fifteen minutes memorization. Thirty minutes recall.
Twelve faces are shown alongside their first name and last names. You have to memorize as many names as you can in fifteen minutes. Spell a name incorrectly and you lose a point!

2. Binary numbers. Thirty minutes memorization. Sixty minutes recall.
Remember as many 0s and 1s in rows of thirty as you can. A one-digit mistake reduces your score to 15 out of 30. Two or more incorrect digits mean you score 0.

3. One-hour numbers. Sixty minutes memorization. Two hours recall.

Numbers are presented in rows of forty digits. One digit wrong scores 20 out of 40. Two incorrect numbers mean you score 0.

4. Abstract images. Fifteen minutes memorization. Thirty minutes recall.

Five abstract images are displayed per row for a total of ten rows per page. For a correct row you get 5 points. A mistake means a deducted point.

5. Speed numbers. Five minutes memorization. Fifteen minutes recall.

Digits are presented in rows of forty. A one-digit mistake means you score 20. Two or more mistakes mean you score 0.

6. Historic/future dates. Five minutes memorization. Fifteen minutes recall.

Made-up dates are presented on multiple pages to be memorized. Points are given for correct date recall and deductions for mistakes made.

7. One-hour cards. Sixty minutes memorization. Two hours recall.

You can select as many decks of cards as you can memorize in one hour. Results can vary from no decks memorized up to a whopping thirty decks!

8. Random words. Fifteen minutes memorization. Thirty minutes recall.

Four hundred words are presented in rows of twenty. Get one word incorrect and you score 10 out of 20. Two or more incorrect words mean you score 0.

9. Spoken numbers. 200, 300, and 400 seconds. Up to twenty minutes recall.
Digits of numbers are spoken by an official at one-second intervals for 200, 300, and 400 seconds. The person who has memorized the most consecutive numbers in a row from the very beginning wins the event.

10. Speed cards. Five minutes memorization. Five minutes recall.
This is the competition finale. The winner is whoever can memorize a deck of randomly shuffled cards within five minutes. The current record (at time of writing) stands at 20.44 seconds by Simon Reinhard of Germany.

So the memory competition is not just about who can memorize the most, but who can memorize the most, most effectively, and fastest. My experience as a mental athlete helps me enormously when teaching others how to memorize effectively, without the need to go back and repeat again and again.

It's interesting, too, that the more I learned about memory, the more I got from speed-reading—and vice versa. To help explain this let's turn to the speed numbers event of the Memory Championships.

Speed-Reading and Memory: The Essential Link
There are various ways of using the Major System to memorize a row of forty digits. One way is to memorize two digits per location, giving you twenty stories per line of forty digits.

Location 1	Location 2	Location 3	Location 4
Front door	Couch	TV	Window
(17)	(23)	(97)	(67)

The story for the previous can be something like this:

A dog (17) bites the front door (location 1).

A gnome (23) jumps up and down on the couch (location 2).

A bike (97) is ridden into the TV (location 3).

Chocolate (67) is smothered all over the window (location 4).

Now, most people could remember these stories if they spent time imagining them. But with only a few seconds to memorize them, you may forget part of a story, which means forgetting the number. And as there are twenty short stories to remember in a row of forty digits, there is a high possibility of making one mistake, or even two, out of that twenty.

To reduce this risk my approach was to memorize four digits at one location. This means ten stories to remember for each forty digits.

Location 1	Location 2	Location 3	Location 4
Front door	Couch	TV	Window
(17 23)	(97 67)	(21 01)	(39 40)

The story can now be something like this:

A dog (17) bites a gnome's (23) bottom at the front door (location 1).

A bike (97) was painted with chocolate (67) on top of the couch (location 2).

A net (21) was wrapped around a seat (01) to smash through the TV (location 3).

A mop (39) was mopping away rice (40) surrounding the window (location 4).

It's a little longer but now there is more of a storyline instead of very short connections using two digits. A storyline is always more effective than a simple link because it has *meaning*. It is much more difficult to create meaning or a storyline for one particular image, and there is simply not enough time in the competition and not enough elements to drive the story further. While these techniques both accomplish the same task in remembering a row of forty digits, the four-digit memorization method is a far more effective strategy.

In fact, it's possible to memorize even more digits in a location. What if you were to try ten? This means making a story with five images linked to one another four times for each row. So if you only have four stories to remember per row of forty digits, chances are you will remember them—especially if your story is imaginative.

So what does this tell us about speed-reading and memory? It tells us that they are essentially the same thing. The more stories we bunch together, the more effective the recall, which is proof of the saying "A picture is worth a thousand words."

The things you need to become memory champion are the same as those needed to excel in any other field, whether it's competitive sports, business, education, or entertainment. They include hard work, self-discipline, sound strategies, supportive, strong, positive people around you, and a genuine passion and love for what you do.

The World Memory Championships Training Program

Here is a program of activities to help you train for the World Memory Championships. For those who don't wish to enter the competition this is still a great brain-training program.

Names and Faces

1. Jump on a site such as Facebook or LinkedIn.
2. Find a page where it displays a list of people's names and their photograph.
3. Memorize their names using SMASHIN' SCOPE through linking and association.
4. Start timing yourself both with memorizing and recall. Try recalling the name by viewing the photograph only, ensuring you cover the name if it's directly under the photo.

Binary Numbers

1. Download binary digits file from *www.tanselali.com*. Or use the two pages of binary code here to make a start.
2. Memorize the following binary code using the Major System or Dominic System for the digits.

000 = 0	100 = 4
001 = 1	101 = 5
010 = 2	110 = 6
011 = 3	111 = 7

3. Memorize the binary code in pairs (as follows) in rows of thirty for five minutes.

100 111 001 010 000 011 111 001 010 010

100 111 (rock), 001 010 (ton), 000 011 (sumo), 111 001 (cat), 010 010 (nun)

As you get better, increase your memorization time from five to ten minutes. Then from ten to twenty minutes.

```
1 0 1 0 0 0 1 1 1 1 1 1 1 0 0 1 0 1 0 0 1 0 1 1 1 0 0 0 0 0
1 1 0 1 0 1 1 1 1 0 0 0 1 1 1 0 1 0 1 1 1 0 0 0 0 1 1 1 1 0
0 0 1 1 0 1 0 1 1 0 1 1 0 0 0 0 1 0 0 0 1 1 1 1 0 0 1 1 0
0 1 0 0 0 1 1 1 1 0 0 0 0 1 1 0 0 1 0 0 0 1 0 0 1 1 1 1 1 1
0 1 1 0 1 1 1 0 1 1 1 0 1 0 0 0 1 1 0 0 1 0 0 0 0 0 1 0 1 1
0 1 1 0 1 0 1 1 0 0 0 0 1 0 0 0 0 1 1 0 1 0 1 1 0 0 0 1 1 1
0 1 1 0 1 1 0 0 1 0 1 1 0 1 0 1 0 0 1 0 1 1 1 1 1 1 1 0 1 1
1 0 1 1 1 0 0 0 0 1 1 0 1 0 1 0 0 0 1 0 1 0 0 1 0 1 0 0 0 0
1 0 1 0 0 0 0 1 0 0 0 0 0 0 1 1 1 0 0 1 0 0 0 1 1 0 1 1 0
0 0 0 1 1 0 0 0 0 0 1 0 0 1 1 0 0 0 1 0 0 1 0 0 1 0 1 1 1 1
0 1 0 0 0 0 1 1 0 0 0 1 1 0 1 0 1 0 0 0 1 1 1 0 1 1 0 0 1 1
0 0 1 0 0 1 0 0 0 1 0 0 1 0 0 1 0 0 1 0 0 1 1 1 0 1 0 1 0 0 0 0 1
0 1 0 0 1 1 1 1 1 0 1 1 1 1 1 1 0 1 0 1 1 0 0 1 0 1 1 0 1 1
1 1 1 1 1 1 1 1 1 1 0 0 0 0 0 1 0 0 0 0 0 0 0 1 1 0 1 0 1 1
1 0 1 1 1 1 1 1 0 0 1 0 0 0 1 1 0 1 1 1 0 1 0 0 1 0 1 1 1 1
0 0 1 1 0 0 1 1 1 0 0 1 1 0 1 0 0 0 1 0 1 0 0 1 1 1 0 1 1 1
1 0 0 1 0 0 0 0 0 0 0 1 0 0 1 1 1 0 0 1 0 0 1 1 0 1 0 1 1
1 1 0 0 1 0 0 0 1 1 1 1 1 1 0 1 1 0 1 0 0 1 0 0 0 1 0 0 0 0
0 1 1 1 0 0 0 0 1 1 0 1 0 1 1 0 0 0 1 0 0 0 0 1 1 1 0 1 0 0
0 0 0 1 0 1 0 0 0 0 1 1 1 0 0 1 1 1 1 1 1 0 0 1 0 0 0 0 0 1
0 1 0 0 1 0 1 1 1 1 0 1 0 1 1 1 1 1 0 1 1 0 1 0 1 0 1 1 1 0
0 0 1 1 0 1 0 0 1 0 1 1 1 1 0 0 1 1 1 1 0 1 1 0 1 0 1 0 0 0
0 1 1 0 0 0 1 1 0 1 1 0 1 1 0 0 1 1 1 0 1 0 1 1 0 1 0 0 1 1
1 1 1 0 1 0 1 0 1 0 0 1 0 0 1 0 1 1 1 1 0 0 0 1 0 0 0 0 0 0
0 0 1 1 1 1 1 0 1 1 1 0 0 1 1 1 1 0 1 0 0 1 0 0 0 0 0 0 0 0
1 0 1 0 0 0 1 1 1 1 1 1 1 0 1 0 0 1 0 1 0 0 1 1 1 0 0 0 0 0
1 1 0 1 0 1 1 1 1 0 0 0 1 1 1 0 1 0 1 1 1 0 0 0 0 1 1 1 1 0
0 0 1 1 0 1 0 1 1 0 1 1 0 0 0 0 1 0 0 0 1 1 1 1 0 0 1 1 0
0 1 0 0 0 1 1 1 1 0 0 0 0 1 1 0 0 1 0 0 0 1 0 0 1 1 1 1 1 1
0 1 1 0 1 1 1 0 1 1 1 0 1 0 0 0 1 1 0 0 1 0 0 0 0 0 1 0 1 1
0 1 1 0 1 0 1 1 0 0 0 0 1 0 0 0 0 1 1 0 1 0 1 1 0 0 0 1 1 1
0 1 1 0 1 1 0 0 1 0 1 1 0 1 0 1 0 0 1 0 1 1 1 1 1 1 1 0 1 1
1 0 1 1 1 0 0 0 0 1 1 0 1 0 1 0 0 0 1 0 1 0 0 1 0 1 0 0 0 0
1 0 1 0 0 0 0 1 0 0 0 0 0 0 1 1 1 0 0 1 0 0 0 1 1 0 1 0 1 0
0 0 0 1 1 0 0 0 0 0 1 0 0 1 1 0 0 0 1 0 0 1 0 0 1 0 1 1 1 1
0 1 0 0 0 0 1 1 0 0 0 1 1 0 1 0 1 0 0 0 1 1 1 0 1 1 0 0 1 1
0 0 1 0 0 1 0 0 0 1 0 0 1 0 0 1 0 0 1 0 0 1 1 1 0 1 0 1 0 0 0 0 1
0 1 0 0 1 0 1 1 1 1 0 1 0 1 1 1 1 1 1 0 1 0 1 1 0 1 1 1 1 0
0 0 1 0 1 0 1 0 0 1 0 1 1 1 1 0 1 1 1 1 1 0 1 1 0 1 0 1 0 0 0
0 1 1 0 0 0 1 1 0 1 1 0 1 1 0 0 1 1 1 0 1 0 1 1 0 1 0 0 1 1
1 1 1 0 1 0 1 0 1 0 0 1 0 0 1 0 1 1 1 1 0 0 0 1 0 0 0 0 0 0
0 0 1 1 1 1 1 0 1 1 1 0 0 1 1 1 1 0 1 0 0 1 0 0 0 0 0 0 0 0
1 0 1 0 0 0 1 1 1 1 1 1 1 0 0 1 0 1 0 0 1 0 1 1 1 0 0 0 0 0
1 1 0 1 0 1 1 1 1 0 0 0 1 1 1 0 1 0 1 1 1 0 0 0 0 1 1 1 1 0
0 0 1 1 0 1 0 1 1 0 1 1 0 0 0 0 1 0 0 0 1 1 1 1 0 0 1 1 0
0 1 0 0 0 1 1 1 1 0 0 0 0 1 1 0 0 1 0 0 0 1 0 0 1 1 1 1 1 1
0 1 1 0 1 1 1 0 1 1 1 0 1 0 0 0 1 1 0 0 1 0 0 0 0 0 1 0 1 1
0 1 1 0 1 1 0 0 1 0 1 1 0 1 0 1 0 0 1 0 1 1 1 1 1 1 1 0 1 1
1 0 1 1 1 0 0 0 0 1 1 0 1 0 1 0 0 0 1 0 1 0 0 1 0 1 0 0 0 0
1 0 1 0 0 0 0 1 0 0 0 0 0 0 1 1 1 0 0 1 0 0 0 1 1 0 1 0
```

```
0 0 0 1 1 0 0 0 0 0 1 0 0 1 1 0 0 0 1 0 1 0 0 1 0 1 1 1 1 1
0 1 0 0 0 0 1 1 0 0 0 1 1 0 1 0 1 0 0 0 1 1 1 0 1 1 0 0 1 1
0 0 1 0 0 1 0 0 0 1 0 0 1 0 0 1 0 0 1 1 1 0 1 0 1 0 0 0 0 1
0 1 0 0 1 1 1 1 1 0 1 1 1 1 1 0 1 0 1 1 0 0 1 0 1 1 0 1 1 1
1 1 1 1 1 1 1 1 1 1 0 0 0 1 0 0 0 0 0 0 1 0 1 0 1 0 0 0 1 1
1 0 1 1 1 1 1 1 0 0 1 0 0 0 1 1 0 1 1 1 0 1 0 0 1 0 1 1 1 1
0 0 1 1 0 0 1 1 1 0 0 1 1 0 1 0 0 0 1 0 1 0 0 1 1 1 0 1 1 1
1 0 0 1 0 0 0 0 0 0 0 1 0 1 1 1 0 0 1 0 0 1 1 0 1 0 1 1
1 1 0 0 1 0 0 0 1 1 1 1 1 0 1 1 1 0 1 0 0 0 1 0 0 0 1 0 0 0
0 1 1 1 0 0 0 0 1 1 0 1 0 1 1 0 0 0 1 0 0 0 0 1 1 1 0 1 0 0
0 0 0 1 0 1 0 0 0 0 1 1 1 0 0 1 1 1 1 1 0 0 1 0 0 0 0 0 0 1
0 1 0 0 1 0 1 1 1 1 0 1 0 1 1 1 1 1 0 1 1 0 1 1 0 1 1 1 1 0
0 0 1 1 0 1 0 0 1 0 1 1 1 1 0 0 1 1 1 1 0 1 1 0 1 0 1 0 0 0
0 1 1 0 0 0 1 1 0 1 1 0 1 1 0 0 1 1 1 0 1 0 1 1 0 1 0 0 1 1
1 1 1 0 1 0 1 0 1 0 0 1 0 0 1 0 1 1 1 1 0 0 0 1 0 0 0 0 0 0
0 0 1 1 1 1 1 0 1 1 1 0 0 1 1 1 1 0 1 0 0 1 0 0 0 0 0 0 0 0
1 0 1 0 0 0 1 1 1 1 1 1 1 0 0 1 0 1 0 0 1 0 1 1 1 0 0 0 0 0
1 1 0 1 0 1 1 1 1 0 0 0 1 1 0 1 0 1 1 1 0 0 0 0 1 1 1 1 0
0 0 1 1 0 1 0 1 1 0 1 1 0 0 0 0 1 0 0 0 1 1 1 0 0 1 1 0
0 1 0 0 0 1 1 1 1 0 0 0 0 1 1 0 0 1 0 0 0 1 0 0 1 1 1 1 1 1
0 1 1 0 1 1 1 0 1 1 1 0 1 0 0 0 1 1 0 0 1 0 0 0 0 0 1 0 1 1
0 1 1 0 1 0 1 1 0 0 0 1 0 0 0 1 1 0 1 0 1 1 0 0 0 1 1 1
0 1 1 0 1 1 0 0 1 0 1 1 0 1 0 1 0 0 1 0 1 1 1 1 1 1 0 1 1
1 0 1 1 1 0 0 0 0 1 1 0 1 0 1 0 0 0 1 0 1 0 0 1 0 1 0 0 0 0
1 0 1 0 0 0 0 1 0 0 0 0 0 0 0 1 1 1 1 0 0 1 0 0 0 1 1 0 1 0
0 0 0 1 1 0 0 0 0 0 1 0 0 1 1 0 0 0 1 0 1 0 0 1 0 1 1 1 1 1
0 1 0 0 0 0 1 1 0 0 0 1 1 0 1 0 1 0 0 0 1 1 1 0 1 1 0 0 1 1
0 0 1 0 0 1 0 0 0 1 0 0 1 0 0 1 0 0 1 1 1 0 1 0 1 0 0 0 0 1
0 1 0 0 1 1 1 1 1 0 1 1 1 1 1 0 1 0 1 1 0 0 1 0 1 1 0 1 1 1
1 1 1 1 1 1 1 1 1 1 0 0 0 1 0 0 0 0 0 0 1 1 0 1 0 0 1 1
1 0 1 1 1 1 1 1 0 0 1 0 0 0 1 1 0 1 1 1 0 1 0 0 1 0 1 1 1 1
0 0 1 1 0 0 1 1 1 0 0 1 1 0 1 0 0 0 1 0 1 0 0 1 1 1 0 1 1 1
1 0 0 1 0 0 0 0 0 0 0 1 0 0 0 0 1 1 1 0 0 1 0 0 1 1 0 1 0 1 1
1 1 0 0 1 0 0 0 1 1 1 1 1 0 1 1 1 0 1 0 0 0 0 0 1 0 0 0 0
0 1 1 1 0 0 0 0 1 1 0 1 0 1 1 0 0 0 1 0 0 0 0 1 1 1 0 1 0 0
0 0 0 1 0 1 0 0 0 0 1 1 1 0 0 1 1 1 1 1 0 0 1 0 0 0 0 0 0 1
0 1 0 0 1 0 1 1 1 1 0 1 0 1 1 1 1 1 0 1 1 0 1 1 0 1 1 1 1 0
0 0 1 1 0 1 0 0 1 0 1 1 1 1 0 0 1 1 1 1 0 1 1 0 1 0 1 0 0 0
0 1 1 0 0 0 1 1 0 1 1 0 1 1 0 0 1 1 1 0 1 0 1 1 0 1 0 0 1 1
1 1 1 0 1 0 1 0 1 0 0 1 0 0 1 0 1 1 1 1 0 0 0 1 0 0 0 0 0 0
0 0 1 1 1 1 1 0 1 1 1 0 0 1 1 1 1 0 1 0 0 1 0 0 0 0 0 0 0 0
1 0 1 0 0 0 1 1 1 1 1 1 1 0 0 1 0 1 0 0 1 0 1 1 1 0 0 0 0 0
1 1 0 1 0 1 1 1 1 0 0 0 1 1 1 0 1 0 1 1 1 0 0 0 0 1 1 1 1 0
0 0 1 1 0 1 0 1 1 0 1 1 0 0 0 0 0 1 0 0 0 1 1 1 1 0 0 1 1 0
0 1 0 0 0 1 1 1 1 0 0 0 0 1 1 0 0 1 0 0 0 1 0 0 1 1 1 1 1 1
0 1 1 0 1 1 1 0 1 1 1 0 1 0 0 0 1 1 0 0 1 0 0 0 0 0 1 0 1 1
0 1 1 0 1 0 1 1 0 0 0 1 0 0 0 1 1 0 1 0 1 1 0 0 0 1 1 1
0 1 1 0 1 1 0 0 1 0 1 1 0 1 0 1 0 0 1 0 1 1 1 1 1 1 0 1 1
1 0 1 1 1 0 0 0 0 1 1 0 1 0 1 0 0 0 1 0 1 0 0 1 0 1 0 0 0 0
1 0 1 0 0 0 0 1 0 0 0 0 0 0 0 1 1 1 1 0 0 1 0 0 0 1 1 0 1 0
0 0 0 1 1 0 0 0 0 0 1 0 0 1 1 0 0 0 1 0 1 0 0 1 0 1 1 1 1 1
0 1 0 0 0 0 1 1 0 0 0 1 1 0 1 0 1 0 0 0 1 1 1 0 1 1 0 0 1 1
0 0 1 0 0 1 0 0 0 1 0 0 1 0 0 1 0 0 1 1 1 0 1 0 1 0 0 0 0 1
0 1 0 0 1 1 1 1 1 0 1 1 1 1 1 0 1 0 1 1 0 0 1 0 1 1 0 1 1
1 1 1 1 1 1 1 1 1 1 1 0 0 0 0 0 1 0 0 0 0 0 1 1 0 1 0 0 1 1
```

One-Hour Numbers

1. Download the random numbers file from *www.tanselali.com.*
2. Memorize six decimal digits per location for twenty minutes, then go back and review for ten minutes. Repeat this process for a total of one hour. There are various ways of doing this. You may prefer to memorize for ten minutes, then go back and review—just don't memorize for one hour straight; you'll become tired and may end up forgetting everything!
3. Memorize numbers in groups of three pairs, and in rows of forty. For the last four digits of each row you can use the Dominic System.

   471203712294634031590948277103566271978
   [471203] [712294] [634031] [590948] [827710] [356627]
   [1978]

It makes sense to use more digits in a location for one-hour numbers so you have fewer stories and locations to remember.

Abstract Images

1. Download samples from *www.tanselali.com.*
2. Memorize by linking each abstract image together in a row of five.
3. Memorize for fifteen minutes straight.
4. Test your recall.

Speed Numbers

1. Download the random numbers file from *www.tanselali.com.*
2. Memorize for five minutes straight using any method you prefer. Five minutes of memorization with no review helps

strengthen your long-term memory and allows you to memorize more. At first you'll make a lot more mistakes but with practice you'll get a whole lot better.

Historic/Future Dates

1. Download the random dates file from *www.tanselali.com*.
2. Memorize as many dates as you can in five minutes using any number system.
3. Here are the sorts of things you're likely to find:

    1971: a cat jumped over the fence.

    2012: a mobile phone floats on water.

    1766: Peter Pan flies over Antarctica.

    1335: the first painting of a chimpanzee is sold to a merchant in France.

    1818: wife divorces husband for forgetting wedding anniversary.

One-Hour Cards

1. Have shuffled decks of cards ready. (The number depends on how many you would like to memorize in an hour.)
2. Download recall sheets from *www.tanselali.com* and print them out.
3. Memorize three cards per location for twenty minutes, then go back and review for ten minutes. Repeat this process for a total of one hour. There are various ways of doing this and you may even choose to memorize four decks, then review and repeat the process.

Random Words

1. Download random words list from *www.tanselali.com*.
2. Practice by memorizing two words per location for fifteen minutes.
3. Spend thirty minutes to recall the memorized words in order.
4. Go back and review your mistakes: visualize them.
5. Memorize again for another fifteen minutes.
6. Repeat step 4 to remove any mistakes.

Spoken Numbers

1. Download the spoken numbers file from *www.tanselali.com*.
2. Press start and, using your number and location systems, memorize as many numbers spoken at one-second intervals as you can.
3. When the numbers have all been spoken, write down as many as you can recall. Recall from the first number onward, because any number not memorized after that is where you stop scoring.

Speed Cards

1. Have two decks of playing cards ready—one deck shuffled and the other deck in suit order.
2. Have a stopwatch ready to time yourself.
3. Start your stopwatch upon memorization of the deck of shuffled cards.
4. Stop the clock once you've finished the memorization.
5. Pick up the ordered deck of playing cards.
6. Start your five-minute timer and rearrange the ordered cards to match the memorized first deck.

7. When five minutes is up, or as soon as you've completed rearranging your ordered deck, put both decks side by side and flip them over, card by card, at the same time. If you have memorized and ordered the deck correctly, the cards should be identical as you flip. If they are not, then you have either made a memorization mistake or memorized from the bottom up, in which case turn the reordered deck upside down and flip both decks over that way.

KEY POINTS

- Memory Championships training can fast-track effective memorization.
- Adding more information to be remembered into one location makes it more memorable.
- Speed-reading and memory engage in the same brain function—converting abstract to image.
- Self-discipline; hard work; and practice, practice, and more practice will make you a memory champion.

PUT YOUR MEMORY TO WORK

"Everything is practice."—Pelé

DID YOU KNOW?

When awake, the human brain produces
enough electricity to power a small light bulb.

CHAPTER 13

PRACTICE YOUR SKILLS

IT'S TIME TO practice your new skills. Build the foundation first by using SMASHIN' SCOPE before applying memory techniques.

SMASHIN' SCOPE

Create stories using the following:

pencil + door + lemons

....

excited + television + leaves

....

exasperated + conundrum + toys

....

fork + windows + shower + web

....

cabinet + excellent + noodles + deluxe

....

disturbance + sensitivity + immaculate + technique

....

forest + computer + brochure + painting + kite

....

diligence + football + absence + playground + cloth

....

fascination + golf + humorous + exhibition + freak

....

intelligence + strictness + beauty + adoration + idiosyncrasy

....

Speed-Reading Test

Have a stopwatch ready and hit start when you begin reading the following article. When you finish, hit stop and record your time. Follow the instructions to get your reading speed in words per minute (wpm).

Misunderstanding Memory Forgotten in Education
Daniel Kilov

The deepest dispute in education is based on a mistake.

In what must be now the most watched talk on the Internet (and thus likely all of human history—what other speech could have ever reached twenty-six million viewers?) Sir Ken Robinson calls for a revolution in the way we are educating children. He calls for a move away from fact-filled curricula and instead champions the teaching of creativity. He does not offer much in the way of a positive vision of what this revolutionary classroom would look like, but others using his talk as a rallying point often speak in terms of "twenty-first-century learning skills" which include information literacy, critical thinking, analysis and creative thinking.

The putative dispute between defenders of fact-based learning and advocates of twenty-first-century thinking skills is however based on a false dichotomy and this dissolves once we understand the relevant science of memory. A synthesis of these views, as we will see below, suggests that the best way to promote twenty-first-century skills is to embrace a 500 B.C. Art of Memory.

Supporters of twenty-first-century learning skills conceive of thinking skills as being, in some important way, beyond the mere accumulation of memorized facts. However, scientific research has determined that memory is central to complex cognitive processes such as thinking and problem solving.

The ability to sift through and critically appraise the value of information in any subject cannot be acquired without a significant body of knowledge in that area. The scientist George Miller demonstrated the importance of background knowledge to the use of reference materials, for instance, by asking a group of students to use a dictionary to learn new words. The results are humorous but clearly demonstrate the pitfalls of the anti-fact philosophy:

"Mrs. Morrow stimulated the soup." (That is, she stirred it up.) "Our family erodes a lot." (That is, they eat out.) "Me and my parents correlate, because without them I wouldn't be here." "I was meticulous about falling off the cliff." "I relegated my pen pal's letter to her house."

If we really want to be able to understand and appraise information that comes our way we cannot be content to just look it up on Google.

Even something like ability in chess, often considered a game of pure reasoning and abstract strategy, depends crucially on memory. Herbert Simon, whose research in this area won him a Nobel Prize, demonstrated in a series of experiments that a player's chess ability relied not on IQ or raw mental processing power but on that player's memory bank of typical chess positions and sequences.

In these experiments, players of various levels were shown different configurations of boards from high-level chess games. The participants were then asked to reconstruct the boards from memory. The results were astonishing. Chess experts were able to recall the configurations of the chess pieces almost perfectly. Novice players could only recall about a third of the pieces. The reason for this is that the expert chess players saw the board in a completely different way. Their vast memories of previous chess games meant that the configurations of pieces all had meaning. The superior memory ability of the chess experts was not just a by-product of expertise; it was the essence of their expertise.

For expert players, the source of their skill is what they can remember about a game and the way that those memories influence how they perceive the board in front of them. Similar results have been found across a range of different disciplines.

This should not come as a surprise. No creative idea that has changed the way we view the world has been invented in a vacuum of knowledge: Nobel Prize winners are able to develop their insights only after years spent accumulating knowledge. If their memories of their disciplines were lost to them, say through amnesia, so too would be their creative capacities.

If expert skill, and the creativity it entails, lies in the accumulation of vast stores of knowledge then anything that is going to increase our capacity to form memories and the speed with which we do it should be treasured. This is true even for those of us without aspirations to become world-class experts. All of our mundane, everyday projects depend crucially on memory. Imagine, for instance, being able to absorb foreign language vocabulary like a sponge, internalizing the words needed to speak a new language in weeks rather than years.

Real-life examples of high-speed learning exist. Every year, athletes gather from all over the world to compete in the World Memory Championships and, every year, they demonstrate startling learning abilities. One competitor at the first World Memory Championships, Bruce Balmer, taught himself 2,000 foreign words in a single day. Another competitor from the 1999 World Memory Championships famously taught himself Icelandic in only one week and then went on a talk show in that language. The most remarkable thing about these competitors, however, is that there is nothing special about them at all. Rather, they all employ a small set of simple techniques, known collectively as the Art of Memory.

The techniques of the Art of Memory originated over two thousand years ago in Ancient Greece. These techniques were almost universally practiced by the thinkers of the ancient world who believed that mnemonic training was essential to the cultivation of one's memory, focus and creativity. Creativity was an act of synthesis that could only occur within the mental playground of a trained mnemonist. Appropriately, in Greek mythology, Mnemosyne, the goddess of memory, was the mother of the muses, the goddesses of creativity.

These techniques formed the cornerstone of Western education and were employed and advocated by thinkers like Thomas Aquinas, Petrarch, Giordano Bruno, [Francis] Bacon, [Gottfried] Leibniz and [René] Descartes. For most of the history of education, the view of memorization was one entirely alien to those of us concerned with so-called twenty-first-century learning skills. The deepest dispute in modern educational debate is based on a mistake: If we really want to promote the abilities of critical reasoning and creativity then we would do well to recognize that the right place for the art of memory is not in memory competitions or in history books but in our classrooms and workplaces.

Stop timer! 1,040 words

Divide 1,040 by the time it took you to read: e.g. $1,040 \div 5$ minutes = 208 WPM.

Languages

Memorize how to greet people in other languages.

Amharic (Ethiopia)	tadiyass (hello, informal), teanastëllën (hello, formal)
Arabic	marhaban (hello, informal)
Armenian	barev (hello, informal)
Adnyamathanha (South Australia)	nhangka, nhangka warntu? (how are you?)
Kalaw Lagaw Ya (Torres Strait, Australia)	yawa, ngi midh? (how are you?)
Pitjantjatjara (Central Australia)	wai, wai palya? (how are you?)
Wiradjuri (New South Wales, Australia)	yiradhu marang, yamandhu marang? (how are you?)
Bengali (India)	namaskar (hello)
Bulgarian	zdraveite (hello, pron. *zdrah veytej*)
Chinese	Cantonese: nei ho or lei ho (hello, pron. *ne ho* or *lay ho*); Mandarin: nǐ hǎo (hello, pron. *nee how*); tone is very important
Croatian	bok (hello, informal), dobro jutro (good morning), dobar dan (good day), dobra večer (good evening), laku noć (goodnight)
Czech	dobrý den (hello, formal), ahoj (hello, informal; pron. *ahoy*)
Danish	hej (hello, informal; pron. *hi*), goddag (good day, formal)
Dhivehi (Maldives)	haalu kihineh (how are you?, formal), kihineh (how are you?, informal)
Dutch	hoi (hi, very informal), hallo (hello, informal), goedendag (good day, formal)
Dzongkha (Bhutan)	kuzu zangpo (hello, informal), kuzu zangpo la (hello, formal)
Estonian	tere päevast (good day)

Fijian	bula (hello, informal), bula vinaka (hello, formal)
Finnish	moi, terve, or hei (hello, informal); mitä kuuluu? (how are you?)
French	allo (hello, informal), bonjour (hello, formal), bonsoir (good evening)
Gaelic	dia duit (informal, literally "God be with you")
Georgian	gamarjoba (hello, informal)
German: traditional	hallo (hello, informal), guten Tag (good day, formal), Tag (hello, very informal)
German: Austrian and Bavarian	grüß Gott (hello, formal; pron. *gruess got*), servus (hello, informal; pron. *zair-voos*)
Greek	yassou (hello, informal; pron. *yah-soo*), yassas (plural or formal; pron. *yah-sas*), kaliméra (good morning), kalispéra (good afternoon; pron. *kalee-spe-ra*h)
Gujarati (India)	namaste or kemcho (hello)
Hawaiian	aloha (hello)
Hebrew	shalom (hello, goodbye, peace), ma kore? (informal, what's happening?)
Hindi	namaste (hello)
Indonesian	halo (hello), selamat pagi (good morning), selamat siang (good afternoon), selamat malam (good evening)
Italian	buon giorno (good morning, pron. *bwohn geeornoh*), buon pomeriggio (good afternoon, pron. *bwohn poh-meh-reejee-oh*), buona sera (good evening, pron. *bwohna sehrah*)
Japanese	ohayō (hello, informal), ohayō gozaimasu (good morning), konnichiwa (good afternoon), konbanwa (good evening)
Konkani (Goa, India)	namaskar (hello, informal), namaskaru (formal); dev baro dis div (informal)
Korean	annyeonghaseyo (hello, how are you?)
Latin	salve (sing., pron. *sal-way*), salvete (pl., pron. *sal-way-tay*), ave (sing., formal, pron. *ar-way*), avete (pl., formal, pron. *ar-way-tay*)

Maltese	merħba (welcome), bonġu (good morning), bonswa or il-lejl it-tajjeb (good evening)
Maori	kia ora (hi, informal), tene koe (hello, sing., formal), morena (good morning)
Marwari (India)	khamma ghani, ram ram sa
Persian (Farsi)	salaam (hello, informal, literally meaning "peace")
Pig Latin	eyhay (informal), ellohay (formal)
Polish	cześć (hi, informal; pron. *cheshch*), dzień dobry (hello, good day, good morning, formal; pron. *jeyn dob-ry*)
Portuguese	oi (hi, informal), olá (hello, informal), bom dia, bons dias (good morning, good day; sing./pl.); boa noite or boas noites (good evening, good night; sing./pl.)
Punjabi (India, Pakistan)	sat sri akal (Sikh greeting)
Romanian	(hello, informal), bună dimineata (good morning), bună ziua (good day), bună seara (good evening)
Russian	privet (hello, informal; pron. *pree-vyet*), zdravstvuyte (formal, pron. *zdra-stvooy-tyeh*)
Samoan	mālō (hello, informal), tālofa (hello, formal)
Spanish	hola (pron. *o-la*), buenos días (good morning), buenas tardes (good afternoon), buenas noches (goodnight)
Swahili (Tanzania, Kenya)	habari (informal greeting)
Urdu	ādāb (literally "salutation"), salām (informal), assalām alaikum (formal Muslim greeting)

Memorize more Chinese Mandarin phrases.

Pinyin	English
Bāng wǒ yíxià.	Give me a hand.
Yìzhí wǎng qián zǒu.	Go right ahead.
Lǚtú yúkuài.	Have a good trip.
Zhù nǐ yì tiān guò de yúkuài.	Have a nice day.
Zài lái yígè.	Have another one.
Nǐ zuò wán le ma?	Have you finished?
Tā méi kòng.	He doesn't have time.
Tā xiànzài yǐjīng zài lù shàng le.	He is on his way.
Nǐ hǎo ma?	How are you?
Nǐ yào dāi duōjiǔ?	How long are you staying?
Duōshǎo qián?	How much?
Wǒ duì tā zháomí le.	I am crazy about her.
Wǒ zài làngfèi shíjiān.	I am wasting my time.
Wǒ néng zuò.	I can do it.
Wǒ jiǎnzhí bùnéng xiāngxìn.	I can't believe it.
Wǒ bù néng zài děng le.	I can't wait.
Wǒ méi shíjiān le.	I don't have time.
Wǒ yī gè rén dōu bú rènshi.	I don't know anybody.
Wǒ bù xǐhuan.	I don't like it.
Wǒ rènwéi búshì.	I don't think so.
Wǒ gǎnjué hǎo duō le.	I feel much better.
Wǒ zhǎo dào le.	I found it.
Wǒ tǎoyàn nǐ!	I hate you!
Wǒ xīwàng rúcǐ.	I hope so.
Wǒ zǎo zhīdào le.	I knew it.
Wǒ ài nǐ.	I love you.

Pinyin	English
Wǒ zhùyì dào le.	I noticed that.
Wǒ míngbái le.	I see.
Wǒ rènwéi shì zhèyàng de.	I think so.
Wǒ xiǎng gēn tā shuō huà.	I want to speak with him.
Wǒ yíng le.	I won.
Qǐng gěi wǒ yì bēi kāfēi.	I would like a cup of coffee, please.
Wǒ è sǐ le.	I'm hungry.
Wǒ yào zǒu le.	I'm leaving.
Duì bu qǐ.	I'm sorry.
Wǒ xíguàn le.	I'm used to it.
Wǒ huì xiǎngniàn nǐ de.	I'll miss you.
Wǒ shìshì kàn.	I'll try.
Wǒ hěn wúliáo.	I'm bored.
Wǒ hěn máng.	I'm busy.
Wǒ wán de hěn kāixīn.	I'm having fun.
Wǒ zhǔnbèi hǎo le.	I'm ready.
Wǒ míngbái le.	I've got it.
Zhēnshì nányǐ zhìxìn!	It's incredible!
Hěn yuǎn ma?	Is it far?
Méiguānxi.	It doesn't matter.
Wén qǐlái hěn xiāng.	It smells good.
Shì shíhou le.	It's about time.
Méi shìr.	It's all right.
Hěn jiǎndān.	It's easy.
Hěn hǎo.	It's good.
Lí zhè hěn jìn.	It's near here.
Méi shénme.	It's nothing.

Pinyin	English
Gāi zǒu le.	It's time to go.
Nà shì bùtóng de.	It's different.
Hěn yǒuqù. (very informal)	It's funny.
Nà shì bù kěnéng de.	It's impossible.
Hái xíng.	It's not bad.
Bù nán.	It's not difficult.
Bù zhí dé.	It's not worth it.
Hěn míngxiǎn.	It's obvious.
Háishì yíyàng de.	It's the same thing.
Lún dào nǐ le.	It's your turn.
Wǒ yě yíyàng.	Me too.
Hái méiyǒu.	Not yet.
Fàngsōng!	Relax!
Míngtiān jiàn.	See you tomorrow.
Tā shì wǒ zuì hǎo de péngyǒu.	She is my best friend.
Tā zhēn cōngmíng.	She is so smart.
Màn diǎnr!	Slow down!
Gàosu wǒ.	Tell me.
Duō xiè.	Thank you very much.
Zhè yàng de shìqíng jīngcháng fāshēng.	That happens.
Gòu le.	That's enough.
Hěn yǒuqù.	That's interesting.
Duì le.	That's right.
Zhè shì zhēn de.	That's true.
Zhèlǐ rén hěnduō.	There are too many people here.
Tāmen hùxiāng qīngmù.	They like each other.
Kǎolǜ yí xià.	Think about it.

Pinyin	English
Tài zāogāo la!	Too bad!
Děng děng wǒ.	Wait for me.
Nǐ shuō shénme?	What did you say?
Nǐ rènwéi zěnyàng?	What do you think?
Tā zài shuō xiē shénme?	What is he talking about?
Duō huài de tiānqì!	What terrible weather!
Zěnme la?	What's going on/happening/the problem?
Jīntiān jǐ hào?	What's the date today?
Nǐ qù nǎ lǐ?	Where are you going?
Tā zài nǎ lǐ?	Where is he?
Nǐ tài xìngjí le.	You are impatient.
Nǐ kàn shàngqù hěn lèi.	You look tired.
Nǐ ràng wǒ dà chī yì jīng.	You surprise me.
Nǐ fēngle.	You're crazy.
Bié kèqi.	You're welcome.
Nǐ zǒng shì duì de.	You're always right.
Nǐ de xīnqíng bù hǎo.	You're in a bad mood.
Nǐ zài sāhuǎng.	You're lying.
Nǐ cuòle.	You're wrong.
Wasài!	Wow!

Memorize more French phrases.

French	English
Comment allez-vous?	How are you?
Tout à coup.	All of a sudden.
Tu m'étonnes.	Tell me something I don't know.
Quand on parle du loup.	Speak of the devil.
Je n'ai pas les moyens.	I can't afford it.
Tu te rends compte?	Can you believe that?
Je n'en veux pas.	I don't want it.
Vous essayez de m'avoir.	You're cheating me.
Je ne suis pas intéressé.	I'm not interested.
D'accord, je la prends.	Okay, I'll take it.
Revenons à nos moutons.	Let's get back to the subject at hand.
Pourrais-je avoir un sac?	Can I have a bag?
Je n'ai fait rien de mal.	I haven't done anything wrong.
C'est une erreur.	It was a misunderstanding.
Où m'emmenez-vous?	Where are you taking me?
Tu m'as tellement manqué!	I missed you so much!
À plus tard.	See you later.
Vous êtes très gentil.	You're very kind.
Il faut que je parte.	I have to go.
Je reviens tout de suite.	I will be right back.
Je n'en sais rien.	I have no idea.
J'arrive!	I'm on my way!
Qu'est-ce que c'est?	What is this?
Que faites-vous dans la vie?	What do you do for a living?
Allez!	Oh, c'mon!
J'ai faim.	I'm hungry.

French	English
J'ai le cafard.	I'm feeling down.
Tu t'en sors?	You managing okay?
Je n'en crois pas mes yeux.	I can't believe my eyes.
J'en mettrais ma main au feu.	I'd bet my life on it.
Allez savoir pourquoi.	Your guess is as good as mine.
Ça vous dit?	Are you up for it?
Ça te changera les idées.	It'll take your mind off things.
N'importe quoi!	That's nonsense!
Ca vous plaît?	Do you like it?
J'espère que c'est vrai.	I hope that is true.
Quelle heure est-il?	What time is it?
Donne-moi ça.	Give me this.
Qu'est-ce qui ne va pas?	What is wrong?
Ce n'est pas ma faute.	It's not my fault.
Ça ne fait rien.	Never mind, it doesn't matter.
Ce n'est pas terrible.	It's not that great.
Je suis perdu.	I'm lost.
Sans blague.	Seriously, all kidding aside.
Aidez-moi, s'il vous plaît.	Please help me.
Tiens!	Here you go! (when giving something)
Vraiment!	Really!
Regarde!	Look!
Dépêche-toi!	Hurry up!
Je vais vous aider.	I am going to help.
Vous pouvez marcher?	Can you walk?
Vous pouvez manger tout seul?	Can you feed yourself?
J'ai mal!	It hurts!

French	English
C'est dangereux.	It's dangerous.
Faites attention!	Take care!
C'est froid.	It's cold.
C'est chaud.	It's hot.
N'allez pas par là!	Don't go this way!
Arrêtez!	Stop that!
Laissez-moi tranquille!	Give me a break!/Leave me alone!
Je ne l'ai pas fait intentionnellement.	I didn't do it on purpose.
Ce n'est pas ma faute.	This is not my fault.
Faites-le vous-même.	Do it yourself.
Tu es completement débile.	You're a complete moron.
Quelle genre de nourriture aimes-tu?	What kind of food do you like?
Où suis-je?	Where am I?
Avez-vous de la monnaie, s'il vous plaît?	Do you have change, please?
Quelle est la date aujourd'hui?	What's the date today?
De quel pays viens-tu?	What country are you from?
Nous ne parlons pas chinois.	We can't speak Chinese.
Je suis étudiant.	I am a student.
C'est dans quelle rue?	In which street is it?
Je parle anglais.	I speak English.
C'est la vie!	That's life!
Bon voyage!	Have a good trip!
Vous avez un plan?	Do you have a map?
Tu fais quoi?	What are you doing?
Tu pars quand?	When are you leaving?
Comment tu t'appelles?	What is your name?

French	English
Quel âge as-tu? (formal) Tu as quel âge? (informal)	How old are you?
Je voudrais l'addition, s'il vous plait.	I would like the bill, please.
Je préfère du fromage blanc.	I prefer fresh cheese.
Je suis perdu. Pouvez-vous m'aider, s'il vous plaît?	I am lost. Can you help me, please?
Où sont les taxis, s'il vous plaît?	Where are the taxis, please?
Combien je vous dois?	How much do I owe you?
Combien ça coûte?	How much does that cost?
Fais de beaux rêves.	Sweet dreams.
Quoi de neuf?	What's new?
Ça n'est pas grave!	No problem!
Pas grand chose.	Nothing much.
Un moment s'il vous plaît.	One moment, please.
Viens avec moi!/ Venez avec moi! (polite)	Come with me!

Countries and Their Capital Cities

A		
Afghanistan: Kabul	Albania: Tiranë	Algeria: Algiers
Andorra: Andorra la Vella	Angola: Luanda	Antigua and Barbuda: Saint John's
Argentina: Buenos Aires	Armenia: Yerevan	Australia: Canberra
Austria: Vienna	Azerbaijan: Baku	
B		
Bahamas: Nassau	Bahrain: Manama	Bangladesh: Dhaka
Barbados: Bridgetown	Belarus: Minsk	Belgium: Brussels
Belize: Belmopan	Benin: Porto-Novo	Bhutan: Thimphu
Bolivia: Sucre	Bosnia and Herzegovina: Sarajevo	Botswana: Gaborone
Brazil: Brasília	Brunei: Bandar Seri Begawan	Bulgaria: Sofia
Burkina Faso: Ouagadougou	Burundi: Bujumbura	
C		
Cambodia: Phnom Penh	Cameroon: Yaoundé	Canada: Ottawa
Cape Verde: Praia	Central African Republic: Bangui	Chad: N'Djamena
Chile: Santiago	China: Beijing	Colombia: Bogotá
Costa Rica: San José	Côte d'Ivoire: Yamoussoukro	Croatia: Zagreb
Cuba: Havana	Cyprus: Nicosia	Czech Republic: Prague
D		
Democratic Republic of the Congo: Kinshasa	Denmark: Copenhagen	Djibouti: Djibouti
Dominica: Roseau	Dominican Republic: Santo Domingo	

E		
Ecuador: Quito	Egypt: Cairo	El Salvador: San Salvador
Equatorial Guinea: Malabo	Eritrea: Asmara	Estonia: Tallinn
Ethiopia: Addis Ababa		
F		
Federated States of Micronesia: Palikir	Fiji: Suva	Finland: Helsinki
France: Paris		
G		
Gabon: Libreville	Gambia: Banjul	Georgia: Tbilisi
Germany: Berlin	Ghana: Accra	Greece: Athens
Grenada: Saint George's	Guatemala: Guatemala City	Guinea: Conakry
Guinea-Bissau: Bissau	Guyana: Georgetown	
H		
Haiti: Port-au-Prince	Honduras: Tegucigalpa	Hungary: Budapest
I		
Iceland: Reykjavík	India: New Delhi	Indonesia: Jakarta
Iran: Tehran	Iraq: Baghdad	Ireland: Dublin
Israel: Jerusalem	Italy: Rome	
J		
Jamaica: Kingston	Japan: Tokyo	Jordan: Amman
K		
Kazakhstan: Astana	Kenya: Nairobi	Kiribati: South Tarawa
Kuwait: Kuwait City	Kyrgyzstan: Bishkek	

L		
Laos: Vientiane	Latvia: Riga	Lebanon: Beirut
Lesotho: Maseru	Liberia: Monrovia	Libya: Tripoli
Liechtenstein: Vaduz	Lithuania: Vilnius	Luxembourg: Luxembourg City
M		
Macedonia: Skopje	Madagascar: Antananarivo	Malawi: Lilongwe
Malaysia: Kuala Lumpur	Maldives: Malé	Mali: Bamako
Malta: Valletta	Marshall Islands: Majuro	Mauritania: Nouakchott
Mauritius: Port Louis	Mexico: Mexico City	Moldova: Chişinău
Monaco: Monaco	Mongolia: Ulaanbaatar	Montenegro: Podgorica
Morocco: Rabat	Mozambique: Maputo	Myanmar: Naypyidaw
N		
Namibia: Windhoek	Nauru: Yaren District	Nepal: Kathmandu
Netherlands: Amsterdam	New Zealand: Wellington	Nicaragua: Managua
Niger: Niamey	Nigeria: Abuja	North Korea: Pyongyang
Norway: Oslo		
O		
Oman: Muscat		
P		
Pakistan: Islamabad	Palau: Ngerulmud	Panama: Panama City
Papua New Guinea: Port Moresby	Paraguay: Asunción	Peru: Lima
Philippines: Manila	Poland: Warsaw	Portugal: Lisbon

Q		
Qatar: Doha		
R		
Republic of the Congo: Brazzaville	Romania: Bucharest	Russia: Moscow
Rwanda: Kigali		
S		
Saint Kitts and Nevis: Basseterre	Saint Lucia: Castries	Saint Vincent and the Grenadines: Kingstown
Samoa: Apia	San Marino: San Marino	São Tomé and Príncipe: São Tomé
Saudi Arabia: Riyadh	Senegal: Dakar	Serbia: Belgrade
Seychelles: Victoria	Sierra Leone: Freetown	Singapore: Singapore
Slovakia: Bratislava	Slovenia: Ljubljana	Solomon Islands: Honiara
Somalia: Mogadishu	South Africa: Bloemfontein, Cape Town, and Pretoria	South Korea: Seoul
Spain: Madrid	Sri Lanka: Colombo and Sri Jayawardenapura Kotte	Sudan: Khartoum
Suriname: Paramaribo	Swaziland: Mbabane	Sweden: Stockholm
Switzerland: Bern	Syria: Damascus	
T		
Taiwan: Taipei	Tajikistan: Dushanbe	Tanzania: Dodoma
Thailand: Bangkok	Timor-Leste (or East Timor): Dili	Togo: Lomé
Tonga: Nuku'alofa	Trinidad and Tobago: Port of Spain	Tunisia: Tunis
Turkey: Ankara	Turkmenistan: Ashgabat	Tuvalu: Funafuti

U		
Uganda: Kampala	Ukraine: Kiev	United Arab Emirates: Abu Dhabi
United Kingdom: London	United States of America: Washington D.C.	Uruguay: Montevideo
Uzbekistan: Tashkent		
V		
Vanuatu: Port Vila	Vatican City: Vatican City	Venezuela: Caracas
Vietnam: Hanoi		
Y		
Yemen: San'a		
Z		
Zambia: Lusaka	Zimbabwe: Harare	

General Knowledge Questions

1. Who was the legendary Benedictine monk who invented champagne?
2. Name the largest freshwater lake in the world?
3. Where would you find the Sea of Tranquility?
4. What is someone who shoes horses called?
5. What item of outer clothing was named after its Scottish inventor?
6. What type of weapon is a falchion?
7. Which word goes before vest, beans, and quartet?
8. What is another word for lexicon?
9. Name the seventh planet from the sun.
10. Who invented the rabies vaccination?
11. Ringo Starr narrated early seasons of which children's TV series?
12. The hardest substance on the Mohs scale of mineral hardness is diamond. What's the softest?
13. What martial arts name means "gentle way"?
14. What digit does not exist in Roman numerals?
15. *Camellia sinensis* is an evergreen shrub better known as what?
16. Where did George II die?
17. Humans are 10,000 times more sexually active than what other animal?
18. A group of what animal is called a smack?
19. *Citius Altius Fortius* is the motto for what?
20. What animal produces its own suntan lotion?

Answers: 1. Dom Pérignon; 2. Lake Superior; 3. the Moon; 4. farrier, also blacksmith; 5. mackintosh; 6. sword; 7. string; 8. dictionary; 9. Uranus; 10. Louis Pasteur; 11. *Thomas the Tank Engine*; 12. talc; 13. judo; 14. zero; 15. tea; 16. on the toilet; 17. rabbit; 18. jellyfish; 19. the Olympics; 20. hippopotamus.

Questions about Countries

1. Which is the only American state to begin with the letter *p*?
2. Name the world's biggest island that's not Australia.
3. What is the world's longest river?
4. Name the world's largest ocean.
5. What is the diameter of Earth?
6. What is the world's largest mammal?
7. Which four British cities have underground rail systems?
8. Name the famous Spanish capital of Catalonia.
9. Which city was once the imperial capital of Russia?
10. In which country is the port of Fray Bentos?
11. TAP is the national airline of which country?
12. In which country did the turnip originate?
13. Calico cloth was invented in which country?
14. What is the only continent with no native species of ant?
15. Speedskating started in which country?

Answers: 1. Pennsylvania; 2. Greenland; 3. the Amazon; 4. the Pacific; 5. 12,750 kilometers (7,922 miles); 6. blue whale; 7. Liverpool, Glasgow, Newcastle, and London; 8. Barcelona; 9. Saint Petersburg; 10. Uruguay; 11. Portugal; 12. Greece; 13. India; 14. Antarctica; 15. Netherlands.

175

Questions about Films

1. Name the actor who starred in 142 films, including *The Quiet Man*, *The Searchers*, and *Stagecoach*.
2. What is the oldest film in existence, and when was it made?
3. Which actress has won the most Oscars?
4. Which actress said, "Fasten your seatbelts, it's going to be a bumpy night" in *All about Eve*?
5. Name the director of the Lord of the Rings film series.
6. Who played Neo in *The Matrix*?
7. Name the actress whose career began at the age of three, and who went on to star in films such as *Taxi Driver*, *Contact*, and *The Silence of the Lambs*.
8. A movie must play in what city to be eligible for an Oscar?
9. In which film did Humphrey Bogart say, "We'll always have Paris"?
10. What was the first animated film to be nominated for an Oscar?
11. Which author wrote the screenplay to James Bond's *You Only Live Twice*?
12. In which film adaptation of the novel does Jean Valjean appear?
13. James H. Pierce was the fourth and last silent film actor to play which famous character?
14. Which famous actor inspired the creation of Bugs Bunny?
15. What's the name of the 2015 reboot of the Mad Max films?

Answers: 1. John Wayne; 2. *Roundhay Garden Scene*, made in 1888; 3. Katharine Hepburn: four Oscars and twelve nominations; 4. Bette Davis (as Margo Channing); 5. Peter Jackson; 6. Keanu Reeves; 7. Jodie Foster; 8. Los Angeles; 9. *Casablanca*; 10. *Beauty and the Beast*; 11. Roald Dahl; 12. *Les Misérables*; 13. Tarzan; 14. Clark Gable; 15. *Fury Road*.

Questions about Horticulture

1. Which first lady established the Rose Garden at the White House?
2. Name the world-famous gardens found outside of London, close to the River Thames.
3. Which garden is one of the Seven Wonders of the Ancient World?
4. What color is a Welsh poppy?
5. What color is a Himalayan poppy?
6. What flower is the symbol of culture?
7. What tree can be English, American, or Eurasian?
8. Which common flower's buds could also be used as capers?
9. Which kind of bulbs were once exchanged as a form of currency?
10. By which Latin name was *Rosa gallica* previously known?
11. "Moons of the faithful" is the Chinese translation for which fruit?
12. What is the common name of *Eucalyptus microtheca*?
13. What plant has flowers but no leaves?
14. What vegetable gets its name from the word for milk?
15. Elizabeth I had anthophobia. What was she afraid of?

Answers: 1. Ellen Wilson, wife of Woodrow Wilson; 2. Kew Gardens; 3. the Hanging Gardens of Babylon; 4. yellow; 5. blue; 6. lotus; 7. elm; 8. nasturtium; 9. tulips; 10. *Rosa mundi*; 11. apricot; 12. coolibah tree; 13. cactus; 14. lettuce, old French/Latin; 15. flowers, specifically roses.

Questions about Sports

1. What color jersey is worn by the winners of each stage of the Tour de France?
2. Name the only heavyweight boxing champion to finish his career of forty-nine fights without ever having been defeated.
3. What course is the traditional home of golf's Masters?
4. Who is the only player to hit an MLB home run and score an NFL touchdown in the same week?
5. How many times was the Men's Tennis Singles at Wimbledon won by Björn Borg?
6. In 2011, which country hosted a Formula 1 race for the first time?
7. Hockey legend Wayne Gretzky played for what team in the 1980s?
8. Which chess piece can only move diagonally?
9. Which gymnast won three gold medals at the 1976 Olympics?
10. Which NBA star holds the record for three-pointers?
11. Which speedskater was the *Sports Illustrated* Sportswoman of the Year in 1994?
12. Who holds the highest batting average in MLB history?
13. Which golfer has the most PGA golf tour wins?
14. Which NCAA men's basketball team has won the most championships?
15. Which famous Hawaiian is commonly regarded as the father of modern surfing?
16. In which sport are left-handed people banned from playing?
17. What is Usain Bolt's fastest time for the 100 meters?
18. Which two teams played in the first Super Bowl?
19. Which athlete has won the most Olympic medals?
20. How long is a marathon?

Answers: 1. yellow; 2. **Rocky Marciano**; 3. Augusta; 4. Deion Sanders; 5. five; 6. India; 7. Edmonton Oilers; 8. bishop; 9. Nadia Comaneci; 10. Ray Allen; 11. **Bonnie Blair**; 12. **Ty Cobb** (.366); 13. Sam Snead, eighty-two wins; 14. UCLA; 15. Duke Kahanamoku; 16. polo; 17. 9.58 seconds; 18. Green Bay Packers and Kansas City Chiefs; 19. Michael Phelps; 20. 26.2 miles.

Questions about the Arts

1. Name the three primary colors.
2. In needlework, what does UFO refer to?
3. Name the famous Russian ballet dancer who won three Emmys and was nominated for an Academy Award and Golden Globe.
4. What is the painting *La Gioconda* more commonly known as?
5. What does the term "piano" mean?
6. Name the Spanish artist and sculptor famous for cofounding the Cubist movement.
7. How many valves does a trumpet have?
8. Who painted *How Sir Galahad, Sir Bors, and Sir Percival Were Fed with the Sanct Grael; but Sir Percival's Sister Died by the Way*?
9. If you were painting with tempera, what would you be using to bind together color pigments?
10. What is John Leach famous for making?
11. Who said, "I like Beethoven, especially the poems"?
12. What arts movement was founded by Tristan Tzara?
13. What is the bestselling album of all time?
14. Who wrote the popular Harry Potter book series?
15. How big is the painting *Guernica*?

Answers: 1. red, yellow, and blue; 2. an unfinished object; 3. Rudolf Nureyev; 4. *Mona Lisa*; 5. to be played softly; 6. Pablo Picasso; 7. three; 8. Dante Gabriel Rossetti; 9. egg yolk; 10. pottery; 11. Ringo Starr; 12. Dadaism; 13. Michael Jackson's *Thriller*; 14. J.K. Rowling; 15. 11.5 × 25.6 feet.

Questions about History

1. When was William Shakespeare born?
2. Who was Henry VIII's first wife?
3. On what date did Germany invade Poland?
4. Who is credited for creating the first American flag?
5. What year was the United Nations founded?
6. What year did Margaret Thatcher become prime minister of the United Kingdom?
7. When did the Berlin Wall come down?
8. Who is regarded as the founder of Medicare and what year was it introduced?
9. When did the Eurostar train service between Britain and France start running?
10. When was the euro introduced as legal currency on the world market?
11. Which presidents are carved into Mount Rushmore?
12. In what year was the Magna Carta signed?
13. Which constitutional amendment gave women the right to vote?
14. What was the spacecraft's name for the first manned Moon landing?
15. Who did the United States buy Alaska from?
16. Who invented the first polio vaccine?
17. In which year was Nelson Mandela released from prison?
18. What date is France's Bastille Day?
19. Which planet was discovered by William Herschel in 1781?
20. Which U.S. presidents have been assassinated and when?

Answers: 1. April 23, 1564; 2. Catherine of Aragon; 3. September 1, 1939; 4. Betsy Ross; 5. 1945; 6. 1979; 7. November 9, 1989; 8. Lyndon B. Johnson, 1965; 9. November 14, 1994; 10. January 1, 1999; 11. Thomas Jefferson, George Washington, Theodore Roosevelt, and Abraham Lincoln. 12. 1215; 13. Nineteenth Amendment; 14. *Apollo 11*; 15. Russia; 16. Jonas Salk, 1952; 17. 1990; 18. July 14; 19. Uranus; 20. Four: Abraham Lincoln, 1865; James A. Garfield, 1881; William McKinley, 1901; John F. Kennedy, 1963.

Questions about Books

1. What is the oldest surviving printed book?
2. In publishing, what does POD mean?
3. Who were Agatha Christie's two most famous sleuths?
4. Which Shakespeare play features Shylock?
5. Who wrote the novel *To Kill a Mockingbird?*
6. Who wrote *Where the Wild Things Are?*
7. What is an e-book?
8. What is the largest library in the world?
9. What bestselling American history book was written by Howard Zinn?
10. How old is the world's oldest dictionary?
11. Who wrote the plays *Three Sisters* and *The Cherry Orchard?*
12. Which travel writer comes from Des Moines, Iowa?
13. Which author had the middle names Ronald Reuel?
14. Which famous writer said, "There is nothing to writing. All you do is sit down at a typewriter and bleed"?
15. Who is the Head of Hogwarts?
16. Which Nobel Prize–winning author wrote the book *Doctor Zhivago?*
17. What is the second book of the Old Testament?
18. Who invented movable type?
19. Who created the Mary Poppins books?
20. What is the name of Charles Dickens's last book, left unfinished?

Answers: 1. *Diamond Sutra*, dated to A.D. 868; 2. print on demand; 3. Hercule Poirot and Miss Marple; 4. *The Merchant of Venice*; 5. Harper Lee; 6. Maurice Sendak; 7. A book available in a digital (electronic) format; 8. The Library of Congress; 9. *A People's History of the United States*; 10. cuneiform tablets dated to 2300 B.C.; 11. Anton Chekhov; 12. Bill Bryson; 13. J.R.R. Tolkien; 14. Ernest Hemingway; 15. Dumbledore; 16. Boris Pasternak; 17. Exodus; 18. Johann Gutenberg (1440); 19. P.L. Travers; 20. *The Mystery of Edwin Drood.*

Questions about TV

1. In *Thunderbirds*, what was Lady Penelope's chauffeur called?
2. What was *Skippy*?
3. The popular show *American Bandstand* was hosted by which entertainment legend?
4. Which *Sesame Street* resident lives in a trash can?
5. Which long-running animated show features Moe's Tavern?
6. Which 1990s TV show has the slogan "The truth is out there"?
7. Which popular BBC series about old collectibles began in 1977, presented by Bruce Parker and Arthur Negus, and is still running to this day?
8. Which 1980s TV series finale revealed that the entire show had been a dream?
9. What was Barney and Betty's son's name in *The Flintstones*?
10. Which Australian actor was memorably killed off in season 4 of *Game of Thrones*?
11. In what year were the first Emmy Awards presented?
12. Which British actor was the star of the HBO series *Deadwood*?
13. The car in the *Knight Rider* series was called KITT. What does this acronym stand for?
14. Which news program shows a stopwatch in its opening?
15. What was the name of the Lone Ranger's horse?

Answers: 1. Parker; 2. 1960s TV series starring Skippy the kangaroo; 3. Dick Clark; 4. Oscar the Grouch; 5. *The Simpsons*; 6. *The X-Files*; 7. *Antiques Roadshow*; 8. *Newhart*; 9. Bamm-Bamm; 10. Noah Taylor; 11. 1949; 12. Ian McShane; 13. Knight Industries Two Thousand; 14. *60 Minutes*; 15. Silver.

Questions about Food and Drink

1. If you had Lafite-Rothschild on your dinner table, what would it be?
2. What is sushi traditionally wrapped in?
3. May Queen, Gala, Wisley Crab, Honeycrisp, and Lane's Prince Albert are all species of what?
4. What is another name for allspice?
5. What color is absinthe?
6. What flavor is Cointreau?
7. How many hot dogs do Americans consume each year?
8. True or false? Fried tarantulas, eggs boiled just before they're due to hatch, and puffin hearts eaten raw when still warm are all traditional foods.
9. How many crocus flowers does it take to make 500 grams of saffron?
10. What food is found by sniffing pigs or dogs?
11. There are more than 1,500 varieties of what food?
12. In ancient Egypt what food was reserved for the Pharaohs?
13. What type of fish is used in making Worcestershire sauce?
14. Which dessert is also known as "Tuscan trifle"?
15. Cavendish, Orinoco, and lady finger are all varieties of which fruit?
16. What is ceviche?
17. What is a coulis?
18. What is the national dish of Scotland?
19. In Bavaria what is defined as a staple food?
20. *Lycopersicon esculentum* is what common food?

Answers: 1. wine; 2. nori (seaweed); 3. apple; 4. pimento; 5. green; 6. orange; 7. 20 billion; 8. true; 9. up to 75,000; 10. truffles; 11. rice; 12. mushrooms; 13. anchovies; 14. tiramisu; 15. banana; 16. South American dish of marinated raw fish or seafood; 17. fruit or vegetable purée, used as a sauce; 18. haggis; 19. beer; 20. tomato.

Quotes

1. *"The roots of education are bitter, but the fruit is sweet."* Aristotle
2. *"Whatever the mind of man can conceive and believe, it can achieve."* Napoleon Hill
3. *"Strive not to be a success, but rather to be of value."* Albert Einstein
4. *"Two roads diverged in a wood, and I—I took the one less traveled by, and that has made all the difference."* Robert Frost
5. *"I attribute my success to this: I never gave or took any excuse."* Florence Nightingale
6. *"What you seek is seeking you."* Rumi
7. *"I've missed more than 9,000 shots in my career. I've lost almost 300 games. Twenty-six times I've been trusted to take the game-winning shot and missed. I've failed over and over and over again in my life. And that is why I succeed."* Michael Jordan
8. *"The most difficult thing is the decision to act; the rest is merely tenacity."* Amelia Earhart
9. *"Definiteness of purpose is the starting point of all achievement."* W. Clement Stone
10. *"Take care of your body. It's the only place you have to live."* Jim Rohn
11. *"Life is what happens to you while you're busy making other plans."* John Lennon
12. *"The mind is everything. What you think you become."* Buddha
13. *"Twenty years from now you will be more disappointed by the things that you didn't do than by the ones you did do, so throw off the bowlines, sail away from safe harbor, catch the trade winds in your sails. Explore, Dream, Discover."* attributed to Mark Twain
14. *"The most common way people give up their power is by thinking they don't have any."* Alice Walker
15. *"The best time to plant a tree was twenty years ago. The second best time is now."* Chinese proverb

Sports Statistics: The World Series

Teams	Year	Winner	Margin
Boston Americans vs. Pittsburgh Pirates	1903	Boston Americans	5–3
n/a (no postseason played)	1904		
New York Giants vs. Philadelphia Athletics	1905	New York Giants	4–1
Chicago White Sox vs. Chicago Cubs	1906	Chicago White Sox	4–2
Chicago Cubs vs. Detroit Tigers	1907	Chicago Cubs	4–0–1
Chicago Cubs vs. Detroit Tigers	1908	Chicago Cubs	4–1
Pittsburgh Pirates vs. Detroit Tigers	1909	Pittsburgh Pirates	4–3
Philadelphia Athletics vs. New York Giants	1910	Philadelphia Athletics	4–1
Philadelphia Athletics vs. New York Giants	1911	Philadelphia Athletics	4–2
Boston Red Sox vs. New York Giants	1912	Boston Red Sox	4–3
Philadelphia Athletics vs. New York Giants	1913	Philadelphia Athletics	4–1
Boston Braves vs. Philadelphia Athletics	1914	Boston Braves	4–0
Boston Red Sox vs. Philadelphia Phillies	1915	Boston Red Sox	4–1
Boston Red Sox vs. Brooklyn Robins	1916	Boston Red Sox	4–1
Chicago White Sox vs. New York Giants	1917	Chicago White Sox	4–2
Boston Red Sox vs. Chicago Cubs	1918	Boston Red Sox	4–2
Cincinnati Reds vs. Chicago White Sox	1919	Cincinnati Reds	5–3
Cleveland Indians vs. Brooklyn Robins	1920	Cleveland Indians	5–2

Teams	Year	Winner	Margin
New York Giants vs. New York Yankees	1921	New York Giants	5–3
New York Giants vs. New York Yankees	1922	New York Giants	4–0–1
New York Yankees vs. New York Giants	1923	New York Yankees	4–2
Washington Senators vs. New York Giants	1924	Washington Senators	4–3
Pittsburgh Pirates vs. Washington Senators	1925	Pittsburgh Pirates	4–3
St. Louis Cardinals vs. Philadelphia Athletics	1926	St. Louis Cardinals	4–3
New York Yankees vs. Pittsburgh Pirates	1927	New York Yankees	4–0
New York Yankees vs. St. Louis Cardinals	1928	New York Yankees	4–0
Philadelphia Athletics vs. Chicago Cubs	1929	Philadelphia Athletics	4–1
Philadelphia Athletics vs. St. Louis Cardinals	1930	Philadelphia Athletics	4–2
St. Louis Cardinals vs. Philadelphia Athletics	1931	St. Louis Cardinals	4–3
New York Yankees vs. Chicago Cubs	1932	New York Yankees	4–0
New York Giants vs. Washington Senators	1933	New York Giants	4–1
St. Louis Cardinals vs. Detroit Tigers	1934	St. Louis Cardinals	4–3
Detroit Tigers vs. Chicago Cubs	1935	Detroit Tigers	4–2
New York Yankees vs. New York Giants	1936	New York Yankees	4–2

Teams	Year	Winner	Margin
New York Yankees vs. New York Giants	1937	New York Yankees	4–1
New York Yankees vs. Chicago Cubs	1938	New York Yankees	4–0
New York Yankees vs. Cincinnati Reds	1939	New York Yankees	4–0
Cincinnati Reds vs. Detroit Tigers	1940	Cincinnati Reds	4–3
New York Yankees vs. Brooklyn Dodgers	1941	New York Yankees	4–1
St. Louis Cardinals vs. New York Yankees	1942	St. Louis Cardinals	4–1
New York Yankees vs. St. Louis Cardinals	1943	New York Yankees	4–1
St. Louis Cardinals vs. St. Louis Browns	1944	St. Louis Cardinals	4–2
Detroit Tigers vs. Chicago Cubs	1945	Detroit Tigers	4–3
St. Louis Cardinals vs. Boston Red Sox	1946	St. Louis Cardinals	4–3
New York Yankees vs. Brooklyn Dodgers	1947	New York Yankees	4–3
Cleveland Indians vs. Boston Braves	1948	Cleveland Indians	4–2
New York Yankees vs. Brooklyn Dodgers	1949	New York Yankees	4–1
New York Yankees vs. Philadelphia Phillies	1950	New York Yankees	4–0
New York Yankees vs. New York Giants	1951	New York Yankees	4–2
New York Yankees vs. Brooklyn Dodgers	1952	New York Yankees	4–3
New York Yankees vs. Brooklyn Dodgers	1953	New York Yankees	4–2

Teams	Year	Winner	Margin
New York Giants vs. Cleveland Indians	1954	New York Giants	4–0
Brooklyn Dodgers vs. New York Yankees	1955	Brooklyn Dodgers	4–3
New York Yankees vs. Brooklyn Dodgers	1956	New York Yankees	4–3
Milwaukee Braves vs. New York Yankees	1957	Milwaukee Braves	4–3
New York Yankees vs. Milwaukee Braves	1958	New York Yankees	4–3
Los Angeles Dodgers vs. Chicago White Sox	1959	Los Angeles Dodgers	4–0
Pittsburgh Pirates vs. New York Yankees	1960	Pittsburgh Pirate	4–3
New York Yankees vs. Cincinnati Reds	1961	New York Yankees	4–1
New York Yankees vs. San Francisco Giants	1962	New York Yankees	4–3
Los Angeles Dodgers vs. New York Yankees	1963	Los Angeles Dodgers	4–0
St. Louis Cardinals vs. New York Yankees	1964	St. Louis Cardinals	4–3
Los Angeles Dodgers vs. Minnesota Twins	1965	Los Angeles Dodgers	4–3
Baltimore Orioles vs. Los Angeles Dodgers	1966	Baltimore Orioles	4–0
St. Louis Cardinals vs. Boston Red Sox	1967	St. Louis Cardinals	4–3
Detroit Tigers vs. St Louis Cardinals	1968	Detroit Tigers	4–3
New York Mets vs. Baltimore Orioles	1969	New York Mets	4–1

Teams	Year	Winner	Margin
Baltimore Orioles vs. Cincinnati Reds	1970	Baltimore Orioles	4–1
Pittsburgh Pirates vs. Baltimore Orioles	1971	Pittsburgh Pirates	4–3
Oakland Athletics vs. Cincinnati Reds	1972	Oakland Athletics	4–3
Oakland Athletics vs. New York Mets	1973	Oakland Athletics	4–3
Oakland Athletics vs. Los Angeles Dodgers	1974	Oakland Athletics	4–1
Cincinnati Reds vs. Boston Red Sox	1975	Cincinnati Reds	4–3
Cincinnati Reds vs. New York Yankees	1976	Cincinnati Reds	4–0
New York Yankees vs. Los Angeles Dodgers	1977	New York Yankees	4–2
New York Yankees vs. Los Angeles Dodgers	1978	New York Yankees	4–2
Pittsburgh Pirates vs. Baltimore Orioles	1979	Pittsburgh Pirates	4–3
Philadelphia Phillies vs. Kansas City Royals	1980	Philadelphia Phillies	4–2
Los Angeles Dodgers vs. New York Yankees	1981	Los Angeles Dodgers	4–2
St. Louis Cardinals vs. Milwaukee Brewers	1982	St. Louis Cardinals	4–3
Baltimore Orioles vs. Philadelphia Phillies	1983	Baltimore Orioles	4–1
Detroit Tigers vs. San Diego Padres	1984	Detroit Tigers	4–1
Kansas City Royals vs. St. Louis Cardinals	1985	Kansas City Royals	4–3
New York Mets vs. Boston Red Sox	1986	New York Mets	4–3

Teams	Year	Winner	Margin
Minnesota Twins vs. St. Louis Cardinals	1987	Minnesota Twins	4–3
Los Angeles Dodgers vs. Oakland Athletics	1988	Los Angeles Dodgers	4–1
Oakland Athletics vs. San Francisco Giants	1989	Oakland Athletics	4–0
Cincinnati Reds vs. Oakland Athletics	1990	Cincinnati Reds	4–0
Minnesota Twins vs. Atlanta Braves	1991	Minnesota Twins	4–3
Toronto Blue Jays vs. Atlanta Braves	1992	Toronto Blue Jays	4–2
Toronto Blue Jays vs. Philadelphia Phillies	1993	Toronto Blue Jays	4–2
n/a (no postseason played)	1994		
Atlanta Braves vs. Cleveland Indians	1995	Atlanta Braves	4–2
New York Yankees vs. Atlanta Braves	1996	New York Yankees	4–2
Florida Marlins vs. Cleveland Indians	1997	Florida Marlins	4–3
New York Yankees vs. San Diego Padres	1998	New York Yankees	4–0
New York Yankees vs. Atlanta Braves	1999	New York Yankees	4–0
New York Yankees vs. New York Mets	2000	New York Yankees	4–1
Arizona Diamondbacks vs. New York Yankees	2001	Arizona Diamondbacks	4–3
Anaheim Angels vs. San Francisco Giants	2002	Anaheim Angels	4–2

Teams	Year	Winner	Margin
Florida Marlins vs. New York Yankees	2003	Florida Marlins	4–2
Boston Red Sox vs. St. Louis Cardinals	2004	Boston Red Sox	4–0
Chicago White Sox vs. Houston Astros	2005	Chicago White Sox	4–0
St. Louis Cardinals vs. Detroit Tigers	2006	St. Louis Cardinals	4–1
Boston Red Sox vs. Colorado Rockies	2007	Boston Red Sox	4–0
Philadelphia Phillies vs. Tampa Bay Rays	2008	Philadelphia Phillies	4–1
New York Yankees vs. Philadelphia Phillies	2009	New York Yankees	4–2
San Francisco Giants vs. Texas Rangers	2010	San Francisco Giants	4–1
St. Louis Cardinals vs. Texas Rangers	2011	St. Louis Cardinals	4–3
San Francisco Giants vs. Detroit Tigers	2012	San Francisco Giants	4–0
Boston Red Sox vs. St. Louis Cardinals	2013	Boston Red Sox	4–2
San Francisco Giants vs. Kansas City Royals	2014	San Francisco Giants	4–3
Kansas City Royals vs. New York Mets	2015	Kansas City Royals	4–1

Source: *www.baseball-reference.com/postseason/*

Narrative Illustration

Rather than always using mind maps, try to draw some pictures freehand to visually narrate the following article.

Skilled Incompetence

Chris Argyris

"Managers who are skilled communicators may also be good at covering up real problems."

The ability to get along with others is always an asset, right? Wrong. By adeptly avoiding conflict with coworkers, some executives eventually wreak organizational havoc. And it's their very adeptness that's the problem. The explanation for this lies in what I call skilled incompetence, whereby managers use practiced routine behavior (skill) to produce what they do not intend (incompetence). We can see this happen when managers talk to each other in ways that are seemingly candid and straightforward. What we don't see so clearly is how managers' skills can become institutionalized and create disastrous results for their organizations. Consider this familiar situation:

The entrepreneur-CEO of a fast-growing medium-sized company brought together his bright, dedicated, hardworking top managers to devise a new strategic plan. The company had grown at about 45 percent per year, but fearing that it was heading into deep administrative trouble, the CEO had started to rethink his strategy. He decided he wanted to restructure his organization along more rational, less ad hoc, lines. As he saw it, the company was split between the sales-oriented people who sell off-the-shelf products and the people producing custom services who are oriented toward professionals. And each group was suspicious of the other. He wanted the whole group to decide what kind of company it was going to run.

His immediate subordinates agreed that they must develop a vision and make some strategic decisions. They held several long meetings to do this. Although the meetings were pleasant enough and no one seemed to be making life difficult for anyone else, they concluded with no agreements or decisions. "We end up compiling lists of issues but not deciding," said one vice president. Another added, "And it gets pretty discouraging when this happens every time we meet." A third worried aloud, "If you think we are discouraged, how do you think the people below us feel who watch us repeatedly fail?"

This is a group of executives who are at the top, who respect each other, who are highly committed, and who agree that developing a vision and strategy is critical. Yet whenever they meet they fail to create the vision and the strategy they desire. What is going on here? Are the managers really so incompetent? If so, why?

395 words

Guitar Scales Tablature

Practice some scales on the guitar.

A major scale

```
e|---------------------------------------4--5--|
B|----------------------------------5--7-------|
G|-----------------------4--6--7--------------|
D|---------------4--6--7----------------------|
A|--------4--5--7-----------------------------|
E|--5--7--------------------------------------|
```

```
e|--5--4-------------------------------------|
B|--------6--4-------------------------------|
G|-------------7--6--4-----------------------|
D|---------------------7--6--4---------------|
A|----------------------------7--5--4--------|
E|-------------------------------------7--5--|
```

A blues scale pattern

```
e|---------------------------------5--8--|
B|------------------------------5--8-------|
G|----------------------5--7--8------------|
D|----------------5--7--------------------|
A|--------5--6--7-------------------------|
E|--5--8---------------------------------|
```

```
e|--8--5-------------------------------------|
B|--------8--5-------------------------------|
G|-------------8--7--5-----------------------|
D|---------------------7--5------------------|
A|----------------------------7--6--5--------|
E|-------------------------------------8--5--|
```

A major pentatonic scale pattern 2

```
e|------------------------------5--7--|
B|-------------------------5--7--------|
G|--------------------4--6-------------|
D|--------------4--7-------------------|
A|--------4--7------------------------|
E|--5--7-----------------------------|
```

```
e|--7--5-----------------------------|
B|--------7--5------------------------|
G|--------------6--4-------------------|
D|--------------------7--4------------|
A|------------------------7--4--------|
E|------------------------------7--5--|
```

A minor pentatonic scale pattern

```
e|------------------------------5--8--|
B|-------------------------5--8--------|
G|--------------------5--7-------------|
D|--------------5--7-------------------|
A|--------5--7------------------------|
E|--5--8-----------------------------|
```

```
e|--8--5-----------------------------|
B|--------8--5------------------------|
G|--------------7--5-------------------|
D|--------------------7--5------------|
A|------------------------7--5--------|
E|------------------------------8--5--|
```

A harmonic minor scale

```
e|------------------------------------------------|
B|------------------------------------------------|
G|------------------------------------------------|
D|--------------------6--7--6--------------------|
A|----------5--7--8------------8--7--5----------|
```

Passwords and Numbers

Memorize these passwords:

9KSYz6sT	cGVFfMru	cDQw84j8
ZB9FJreC	eGWEGxDu	TLeQUhcw
HNNfRrx9	daLqTrvx	eKxpfWDS
n8c4MSSP	fHNpZqg8	fPp2dZVr
agQDxace	uwjapjuK	2PdTVMtB

Memorize these PINs:

7 5 0 4	5 1 6 2
3 0 9 9	0 5 7 8
4 0 4 3	2 2 7 2
8 6 0 9	3 4 1 9

Memorize these credit card details:

06871698916988
Expiration date: 7/20
Code: 117
PIN: 0442

4913732066730948
Expiration date: 12/19
Code: 481
PIN: 9814

6319340759660136
Expiration date: 1/17
Code: 973
PIN: 6412

6519494067666435

Expiration date: 4/16

Code: 860

PIN: 8876

9916793426815443

Expiration date: 1/11

Code: 211

PIN: 4287

1705946746384619

Expiration date: 9/16

Code: 307

PIN: 5455

Challenges

Now that your memory toolbox of techniques is in good shape, here are a list of challenges for you to consider:

- Mind map a recent issue of a magazine such as *Men's Health* or *Vanity Fair*.
- Memorize twenty decks of playing cards.
- Meet twenty people and remember their names.
- Read a 300-page book in three hours.
- Memorize fifty telephone numbers from your contact list.
- Memorize and present a twenty-minute speech without any notes.
- Planning a trip? Learn 1,500 phrases from a language of your choice.
- Memorize the winners of the Super Bowl.

- Teach yourself to learn another instrument—ukulele or a wind instrument?—in less than forty-eight hours using memory and learning principles from this book.
- Join me as a mental athlete in the World Memory Championships.

KEY POINTS

- Make sure you understand the key memory concepts and techniques *before* attempting the exercises.
- Complete these exercises with a friend to make it more fun.
- Try thinking of other applications for memory now that you're familiar with the techniques.
- Don't give up too easily. What may seem difficult may in fact not be once you get started.

SOURCES

General Brain Training
For memory lessons, community forums, and brain training software try: *www.artofmemory.com.*

For those of you who really want to ramp things up, this website was designed by another memory athlete: *http://memorise.org.*

Learning Tools
With a particular focus on career try: *www.mindtools.com.*

Two other well-known sites in this space are: *www.memrise.com* and *www.khanacademy.org.*

World Memory Championships
See record-breaking memory champion Simon Reinhard in action: *www.youtube.com/watch?v=sbinQ6GdOVk.*

For more information on the World Memory Championships go to: *www.worldmemorychampionships.com*; for World Memory Championship statistics go to: *www.world-memory-statistics.com.*

Mind Mapping

For more information on Mind Maps, go to the founder's website, *www.tonybuzan.com*, or XMind offers its own mind mapping software: *www.xmind.net*.

Speaking to an Audience

Take a look at some of these videos online to see what's possible using narrative illustration:

Illustrator Gavin Blake visually represents Rachel Botsman's book *What's Mine Is Yours: The Rise of Collaborative Consumption*: *www.youtube.com/watch?v=NrA1Q_jYKGLY*.

Gavin Blake's website is: *www.feverpicture.com.au*.

Shape Your Thinking: Brandy Agerbeck at TEDxWindyCity, *www.youtube.com/watch?v=6bCHq1OvGR4*.

Specific Sources as Used in the Book

Study Techniques

Shapes: *http://tutorial.math.lamar.edu/cheat_table.aspx*; *www.mathsisfun.com/area.html*; *www.mathsisfun.com/triangle.html*.

Trigonometry: *http://tutorial.math.lamar.edu/pdf/Trig_Cheat_Sheet.pdf*.

Essay writing: Language and Learning Online: *www.monash.edu/lls/llonline/*; essay writing example: *www.monash.edu.au/lls/llonline/writing/general/essay/sample-essay/index.xml*.

SOURCES

Learning Languages

A great resource for phrases can be found at *wikitravel.org/en/Main_Page*. Just type in the language and then "phrasebook": for example, "Hungarian phrasebook."

The Mandarin phrases in Chapters 9 and 13 come from Dig Mandarin. For a more comprehensive list, go to: *www.digmandarin.com/120-daily-used-short-sentences.html*.

Learning Music

Los Angeles Times article: *articles.latimes.com/2010/mar/01/health/la-he-0301-brain-music-20100301;* also mentioned in: *www.hoffmanacademy.com/blog/best-age-to-begin-piano-lessons/*.

There are so many sites online with a focus on music, including instructional videos, and some will be better or more useful to you than others. Do search to find what suits you best, but these may be a good place to start:

- Virtual Piano: *www.virtualpiano.net*.
- GuitarMasterClass: *www.guitarmasterclass.net*.
- Guitar tablature: *www.ultimate-guitar.com*; *www.guitaretab.com*; *www.guitartabs.cc*.

General Knowledge

There are so many online sites with their own brain teasers and quiz questions. One that's worth checking out is *www.knowquiz.com/doc/10000_questions.pdf*.

ACKNOWLEDGMENTS

I NEVER THOUGHT I'd write a book, let alone two! My hope is that this one also helps people and makes their lives a bit easier. Thank you to my amazing parents and family who have supported me and given me strength ever since I was a child. They have been my greatest inspiration. I thank my dear friends and colleagues that have supported me along my journey. Thank you to Nolan Bushnell for helping me send my message of learning to thousands of people around the world. To my awesome contributors, you guys are amazing individuals doing extraordinary things. Keep at it! To my readers, I appreciate you taking your valuable time to acquire knowledge and better yourself. You're also an inspiration for me to keep doing what I do. And finally thanks to my wife and our three beautiful kids. Love you all. Peace.

ABOUT THE AUTHOR

Tansel Ali is a three-time Australian Memory Champion, international memory expert, and coach, who trains people and organizations to improve memory and increase performance. He frequently appears on television and radio and is featured in Todd Sampson's award-winning ABC documentary *Redesign My Brain*. He may, however, be best known for memorizing Sydney's *Yellow Pages* in only twenty-four days. His first book was *The Yellow Elephant: Improve Your Memory and Learn More, Faster, Better*. Tansel lives in Melbourne with his wife and three children.

Website: *www.tanselali.com*

Twitter: @tanselali

ABOUT THE CONTRIBUTORS

Daniel Kilov is a memory athlete. He was the silver medalist at the 2011 and 2012 Australian Memory Championships. He also broke the Australian record for the abstract images event, having memorized 115 abstract shapes in sequence. Since then, Daniel has become a sought-after speaker and educator, described by the media as one of "the nation's finest thinkers and communicators." He was a speaker at the 2011 Australian Mensa Conference and at two TED conferences in 2012. In 2014 he gave another TED talk and spoke at the Mind and Its Potential conference. Daniel believes that we are all mental athletes and that in today's competitive world we all need to remember more, and be more creative, innovative, and focused.

Julien Leyre is a French-Australian writer, educator, and social entrepreneur. In 2011, he founded the Marco Polo Project, a non-profit organization that explores new models to help people understand China and develop cross-cultural empathy by celebrating literature and language. He's currently completing a PhD at Monash University, mapping the digital ecosystem of Chinese language learning and his website is: marcopoloproject.org.